ROBIN HOOD

Adapted by Laura Dockrill

Music by Hugo White

SAMUEL FRENCH

samuelfrench.co.uk

FOR AMATEUR PRODUCTION ENQUIRIES

UNITED KINGDOM AND WORLD
EXCLUDING NORTH AMERICA
plays@samuelfrench.co.uk
020 7255 4302/01

Each title is subject to availability from Samuel French, depending upon country of performance.

Please note that what is printed may differ to what is presented on stage.

THINKING ABOUT PERFORMING A SHOW?

There are thousands of plays and musicals available to perform from Samuel French right now, and applying for a licence is easier and more affordable than you might think

From classic plays to brand new musicals, from monologues to epic dramas, there are shows for everyone.

Plays and musicals are protected by copyright law, so if you want to perform them, the first thing you'll need is a licence. This simple process helps support the playwright by ensuring they get paid for their work and means that you'll have the documents you need to stage the show in public.

Not all our shows are available to perform all the time, so it's important to check and apply for a licence before you start rehearsals or commit to doing the show.

LEARN MORE & FIND THOUSANDS OF SHOWS

Browse our full range of plays and musicals, and find out more about how to license a show

www.samuelfrench.co.uk/perform

Talk to the friendly experts in our Licensing team for advice on choosing a show and help with licensing

plays@samuelfrench.co.uk   020 7387 9373

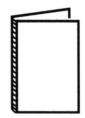

ABOUT THE AUTHOR

Laura Dockrill is an award-winning performance poet and novelist whose wonderfully inventive and vibrant approach to life is reflected in the rich and vividly imagined worlds she creates. Laura grew up in Brixton and attended the Brit School. Laura has always had a vivacious spark, finding creativity in words – from poetry to novels, and scripts to song lyrics.

She is author of the Carnegie Medal nominated YA novel *Lorali, My Mum's Growing Down* (Faber and Faber) as well as the *Darcy Burdock* series (Random House) for younger readers, which was also nominated for the Carnegie Medal and shortlisted for the Waterstones Children's Book Prize in 2014. Other books include *Echoes* (HarperCollins), a collection of poems and short stories.

Laura has appeared on *Blue Peter* and *CBeebies,* and is a frequent poet performer at festivals including Glastonbury, Hay Edinburgh, London Literary Festival and Latitude.

Children's books are at the heart of her work. She curated and wrote both *The Wondercrump World of Roald Dahl* and *Adventures in Moominland* exhibitions at the Southbank Centre, and loves to visit schools and festivals and meet young readers who are as spirited as her.

Laura lives in London and you can follow her on Twitter @LauraDockrill.

AUTHOR'S NOTE

This retelling of *Robin Hood* is a family show using actor/ musicians who are versatile and playful and have a sense of almost improvisation. It is right that the setting of the landscape should be a natural woodland that is wild, overgrown, magical, enchanting and pretty, yet the show has a grotesque, larger- -than-life feel too. Do not be afraid to have fun with the words and music, of course it is a serious piece of work but if you by chance happen to burst into laughter whilst on stage during the performance that is absolutely fine, the atmosphere created should be warm and relaxed and the mood positively infectious. It should feel like a good time.

MUSIC USE NOTE

Licensees are solely responsible for obtaining formal written permission from copyright owners to use copyrighted music in the performance of this play and are strongly cautioned to do so. If no such permission is obtained by the licensee, then the licensee must use only original music that the licensee owns and controls. Licensees are solely responsible and liable for all music clearances and shall indemnify the copyright owners of the play(s) and their licensing agent, Samuel French, against any costs, expenses, losses and liabilities arising from the use of music by licensees. Please contact the appropriate music licensing authority in your territory for the rights to any incidental music.

USE OF COPYRIGHT MUSIC

A licence issued by Samuel French Ltd to perform this play does not include permission to use the incidental music specified in this copy. Where the place of performance is already licensed by the PERFORMING RIGHT SOCIETY (PRS) a return of the music used must be made to them. If the place of performance is not so licensed then application should be made to the PRS, 2 Pancras Square, London, N1C 4AG (www.mcps-prs-alliance. co.uk).A separate and additional licence from PHONOGRAPHIC PERFORMANCE LTD, 1 Upper James Street, London W1F 9DE (www.ppluk.com) is needed whenever commercial recordings are used.

IMPORTANT BILLING AND CREDIT REQUIREMENTS

If you have obtained performance rights to this title, please refer to your licensing agreement for important billing and credit requirements.

SONG LIST

1. I've Always Fancied Myself

2. Robin Hood

3. Outlaws

4. Take These Coins

5. Human Being Ferry

6. Tax Song (Real Nice Guy)

7. We Were Once Friends

8. Proposal Song

9. Double Day

ROBIN HOOD

The Watermill Theatre, first preview 15 November 2018.

Cast list

ROBIN HOOD	Georgia Bruce
FRIAR TUCK/MESSENGER	Jorell Coiffic-Kamall
LITTLE JOHN	Daniel Copeland
SHERIFF OF NOTTINGHAM/ALAN-A-DALE	Leander Deeny
MAID MARION/MISS SNOB	Stephanie Hockley
WILL SCARLET	Ned Rudkins-Stow

Creative list

Director– **Laura Keefe**
Designer – **Frankie Bradshaw**
Lighting Designer – **Ryan Joseph Stafford**
Sound Designer– **Jay Jones**
Musical Director – **Ned Rudkins-Stow**
Composer – **Hugo White**
Movement Director – **Coral Messam**
Fight Choreographer – **Dani Davies**

Production Manager – **Lawrence T. Doyle**
Assistant Production Manager – **Harry Armytage**
Trainee Production Manager – **Eden Harrhy**
Technician –**Tim Knight**
Sound Operator – **Jimmy O'Shea**
Company Stage Manager – **Kerrie Driscoll**
Stage Manager on the Book – **Sara Sandalls**
Rehearsal Deputy Stage Manager – **Alice Barber**
Assistant Stage Managers – **Claire Payton**
Ruth Hills
Natalie Toney
Wardrobe Supervisor – **Emily Barratt**
Wardrobe Assistant – **Louise Patey**
Sign Integrated Performers – **Lixi Chivas & Ana Becker**
Audio Description – **Lixi Chivas**

For Bug

CHARACTERS

MISS SNOB

DRIVER

ROBIN HOOD

LITTLE JOHN

SHERIFF OF NOTTINGHAM

MESSENGER

ALAN-A-DALE

WILL SCARLET

MERRY MANY

BUSY BODY

FRIAR TUCK

MAID MARION

GUARD

ACT ONE

Our story, **ROBIN HOOD,** *is set in a leafy landscape of greenery and shrubbery. The setting is showcasing nature at its best, stuffed with the beauty of the enchanting bewitching woodland; twinkly lights, starry canopies, birdsong, the trickle of the stream, the creaky sounds of the forest, growing and stretching.*

All over the walls of the theatre are 'Reward' posters for **ROBIN HOOD.**

1. A Snobbery!

Characters: **MISS SNOB, DRIVER, ROBIN HOOD, LITTLE JOHN.**

A covered regal carriage trip traps by, glistening under the pale onion of a moon.

LITTLE JOHN, who is not so little, suddenly throws himself in front of the carriage, into the road. The carriage grinds to a halt as it knocks LITTLE JOHN flat down very dramatically. We wait in the dark stillness. Owls hoot.

MISS SNOB *(from inside the carriage)* AHHHHHHHHHH! WATCH IT!

DRIVER WOAH THERE!

MISS SNOB CAN'T YOU DRIVE IN A STRAIGHT LINE YOU WART-FACED WRINKLED WALNUT?

DRIVER My apologies, stay inside miss. Are you alright?

MISS SNOB Not really... I *almost* did a hiccup! What's happened out there anyway?

DRIVER Felt like we hit something.

MISS SNOB No, not *we, Darren,* YOU. You hit something because you're a Giant Great Muffin of a Man that can't keep his head out of a sausage roll packet for two seconds to keep his piggy eyes on the road! Well, did we?

DRIVER Did we what?

MISS SNOB HIT SOMETHING?

DRIVER I don't know, I can't tell, it's so dark I...

MISS SNOB Oh let's not dawdle, drive on Darren.

DRIVER What if it's a person miss?

MISS SNOB MORE the reason to drive on Darren!

DRIVER Miss!

MISS SNOB I'm not going to fork out my precious money for some drunk poor peasant blindly scampering barefoot around the forest who hasn't got the social intelligence to know what a carriage looks like before it hits him flat down racoon-skin dead!

DRIVER I really think we should just check –

MISS SNOB And what about my carriage anyway? Bet that's got a nasty bruise itself. Who will pay for the damage to that then, eh? Me I suppose. Not this penniless lout I tell you that. I'm getting out.

An overly dressed ridiculously eccentric striped stocking and heel pops out of the carriage door...the leg of **MISS SNOB**.

DRIVER No, no, please stay inside miss, it's very dark...and we don't want you, you know...out and about...if it...*is* a person. It won't look good.

MISS SNOB *returns her leg back inside.*

MISS SNOB You're right. For once. You Great Ton of a Toadlette. But you better get us out of this mess. It's getting late, I'm tired and my hair is *not* going to tong itself this evening.

DRIVER *ventures further, creeping in the darkness.*

DRIVER Probably just hit a rabbit. A fox at worst.

The **DRIVER** *gingerly steps forward, closer towards the body.*

MISS SNOB Well, must be a pretty fat fox then, well fed thing, felt more like a bear to me.

DRIVER A badger maybe, perhaps a deer, no bears around here, these woods are very safe.

The **DRIVER** *realises he's hit a human and he's terrified.*

MISS SNOB Knew I should have bought my net. OOoo if it *is* a bear Darren, do chop the head off for me won't you? I've always liked the idea of a bear's head on the dining room wall... You must have an axe somewhere...

> **LITTLE JOHN** *opens one eye and looks terrified. The* **DRIVER** *bravely checks for a pulse on* **LITTLE JOHN**...

HA! A bear's head on the wall...oooo...lovely, lovely... And the paws, they could make mittens! How adorable. Oh and the feet too, for slippers! We could make hats! Matching ones. Darren! We could be twins!

> *And then* **LITTLE JOHN** *rises from 'the dead', and knocks the* **DRIVER** *out with a thump.* **LITTLE JOHN** *then drags the* **DRIVER**'s *body to the side of the road where he begins to snore, deeply.*

Darren? Darren?

LITTLE JOHN Errr...yes? Ma'am... M'lady...or whatever...

MISS SNOB Well IS it a bear or not? Did you get him?

LITTLE JOHN Erm...you *could* say that.

MISS SNOB Oh goody! WE GOT THE BIG BRUTE! Come along then, get going, chop off his head so that we can be on our way.

> **LITTLE JOHN** *sits up at the front of the carriage, the carriage dips with his giant weight.*

You're even HEAVIER! Did you just EAT the thing? Come on...

> *A small slight figure creeps out from the woodland. It's a nimble man dressed in a fine gentleman's suit. He discreetly clambers into the carriage...*

AGHHHHH! WHO ON EARTH ARE YOU?

ROBIN HOOD Have you ever been involved in a serious road accident?

MISS SNOB What the –?

ROBIN HOOD Our systems inform us that, regrettably, you were recently involved in a serious road accident that was NOT your fault.

MISS SNOB Yes, just now, but no need to make a fuss. We just hit some clumsy bear but no damage, thank you, we shall be on our way.

ROBIN HOOD Ahh, sorry to hear that...

MISS SNOB Thank you for your concern...but really we've been away, travelling, I'm awfully tired –

ROBIN HOOD It's just according to our database you could be entitled to compensation –

MISS SNOB By compensation, do you mean *free money*?

ROBIN HOOD You could see it like that, yes...

MISS SNOB How *cute*! I suppose the reality of the accident hasn't quite hit me yet. Still in shock.

ROBIN HOOD I'm sure.

MISS SNOB No, hold on...this is ridiculous, you're having me on, the bear won't have insurance!

ROBIN HOOD No but *you* are protected. There is clumsy wildlife in the woods who ignore road safety.

MISS SNOB TOO RIGHT! I *always* say this. Vehicles come first, *then* nature.

ROBIN HOOD Indeed. You said you've been travelling and I can't help but notice you're loaded with a LOT of luggage, you were putting your fortune at a serious high risk Miss Snob. And for an accident like this, you could be entitled to a rather handsome payout.

MISS SNOB Oh *really*? I suppose I could *try* and relive the incident for the purposes of insurance...

ROBIN HOOD Only if you think you're up to it.

MISS SNOB I'll try my best though I can't make any promises.

ROBIN HOOD I appreciate this must be difficult for you. So...
if you could just give me your name...

MISS SNOB Miss Horaina Sabbatical Nuisance Abacus Snob.

ROBIN HOOD Nuisance with an S or a C?

MISS SNOB With an N you Twit!

ROBIN HOOD Oh sorry, am I troubling you? I can always write
this accident off and leave you to be –

MISS SNOB Oh no, my apologies, I just get angry when I'm
hungry. Hangry. I call it. Do continue...

ROBIN HOOD We will need to take some items, just as *evidence*
of the accident, for our files. I can see here some scratches on
your *gold* and *emerald diamond* watch from the crash. Looks
like some stains on your *velvet* throw here from perhaps a
minor spilling of some tea?

> **ROBIN** *begins to pass items out of the carriage door to*
> **LITTLE JOHN** *who collects them up in a loot bag.*

> Some damage to your rather *expensive* and *rare vintage
> snakeskin purse* and even these *gold* coins inside the purse
> look like they've taken a bashing. And your pearls! I should
> really grab those too. Probably best to take them for evidence
> too.

MISS SNOB Goodness Grief! It really was far worse than I
thought. I'm lucky to be alive.

ROBIN HOOD Yes, but you are in safe hands now.

> **ROBIN** *now pops more of* **MISS SNOB**'s *items out of the
> trap door at the bottom of the carriage, to* **LITTLE JOHN**.
> *A cape, a hat, a handbag –* **LITTLE JOHN** *models the
> winnings.*

MISS SNOB I'm so disorientated... *Where am I? Where am
I?* Excuse my frazzled nerves. I'm so tender from the
experience... I'm really not myself...

ROBIN HOOD I understand Miss Snob. But if you could just try and relay the events...the more detailed, the bigger the compensation. At this stage, with trauma, try *closing your eyes*, that can help the brain to summon up any memories, flashbacks of the crime scene.

MISS SNOB Yes of course. You're quite right. We do this in meditation you see. *Hmm. Maaahhh. Hm –*

ROBIN HOOD Very good, keep the humming going and your eyes *closed*...very nice, very nice.

Objects become more ridiculous with size and opulence, like they couldn't possibly appear from the carriage – in a Mary Poppins' handbag illusion we see umbrellas, rugs, lamps. **LITTLE JOHN** *continues to stuff the bags with loot, whistling with joy, gleefully filling up the sacks.*

MISS SNOB It's all flooding back, it was a dark evening, the owls were hooting, the crickets chirping, the river trickling, the moon...shining...menacing almost with tension...

ROBIN HOOD You might say a night very much like tonight?

MISS SNOB Well of course you might because it *was* tonight you Spot Picking Trout-Faced *Treasure*... I'm sorry, it's my heart, I'm finding it hard to trust anybody... I'm still so delicate... from the crash...see my hand...trembling...?

ROBIN HOOD Not quite, perhaps the shakes are internal?

MISS SNOB *Tonight,* doomsday, when my beloved driver Darren, *with whom as an employer I take excellent first class care of and ensure holiday pay and an ample lunch break,* and I, went from citizens to...a whole new species altogether... *Victims.*

ROBIN HOOD That's very brave of you to admit. So now with your eyes *very tightly shut and perhaps with your back turned* do continue...

MISS SNOB I was just simply minding my own innocent business, coming homeward bound from my travels, I've been on a shopping vacation you see...

ROBIN HOOD Hence the heavy load...

MISS SNOB Well yes...these are not *all* for me of course, most are presents. For the erm...*needy* – when Darren and I were suddenly struck down by what can only be a VIOLENT act of terror!

ROBIN HOOD Keep your eyes closed please Miss Snob, you're doing so well.

MISS SNOB Oh, I'm not sure I can go on. I might need the promise of a new frock or something to comfort me from the trauma, as compensation, to settle my nerves –

ROBIN HOOD Of course Miss Snob.

> **LITTLE JOHN** *poking his head into the trap door underneath the carriage notices some delicious plump cakes he likes the look of, from what we can see he is trying to get* **ROBIN***'s attention, nipping at her heels, pointing towards the treats.* **ROBIN** *is batting him away...*

MISS SNOB And some shoes...they wouldn't hurt...

ROBIN HOOD *(to* **LITTLE JOHN***)* No, you don't need t – STOP being so greedy!

MISS SNOB I beg your pardon? I NEARLY JUST died!

ROBIN HOOD 'STOP BEING SO GREEDY!' *Some other* insurance companies might say, but not me, no. But, still, probably best I take a *few* more bits as evidence.

> *Although we can't see inside the carriage we know that* **ROBIN HOOD** *kicks* **LITTLE JOHN***'s hand away, stamping on it. We see* **LITTLE JOHN** *fall out of the trap door, silently wailing. He then stubs his toe, grunts and it sounds like a fart.*

MISS SNOB Excuse you!

ROBIN HOOD Pardon me. Breaking these kind of deals gets me awfully worked up. If it's one thing I like, it's justice.

MISS SNOB So what about the shoes?

ROBIN HOOD Excellent idea, some nice solid rubber orthopedic durable things, practical ones, to keep you safe, should an accident happen again...

MISS SNOB NO you Bluetitted Anchovy Gobbling House-Fly... to wear with the frock.

ROBIN HOOD Whatever eases your nerves, Miss Snob...

More luxurious food exits the carriage; bread, cheese, wine, pies, cakes and **LITTLE JOHN** *is loving it. A bunch of grapes now slides out of the trap door which* **LITTLE JOHN** *takes in his mouth.*

Now if you could just read this declaration here, including the smallprint and sign, it's just to say you willingly have given us the permission to take your items, leaving them in our total responsibility.

MISS SNOB As evidence of the incident?

ROBIN HOOD Correct. And *almost* done, if you could just write your contact details here...that's great, address and...perfect... and then your bank details down there?

MISS SNOB Why do you need *my* bank details? Isn't the bear paying *me*?

ROBIN HOOD Errrmmm...

MISS SNOB Oh, of course, *duh*, air head, for the compensation pay out.

ROBIN HOOD Exactly. For the compensation pay out. Wow. Have you done this before? So just your sort code *and* account number if you wouldn't mind – that's just lovely, just wonderful and finally – your security code and password please, followed by a pin number...it should be about four digits long?

MISS SNOB I know I look *scarily* young but do you think I was born yesterday?

ROBIN HOOD Not for a SECOND Miss Snob!

MISS SNOB If you think I'm giving out my personal details to some strange roadsman then I'm afraid you have another think coming, you can take this matter up with my lawyers, thank you and goodbye. Darren, let's be getting a wiggle on please...

LITTLE JOHN *jumps to attention at the carriage wheel.*

LITTLE JOHN Err... Yes...m'lady...ma'am...maaaaaaa...

LITTLE JOHN, *too into character, almost goes to drive away,* **ROBIN** *has to stop him.* **ROBIN HOOD** *and* **LITTLE JOHN**, *having what they need, are quick to leave the crime scene.*

ROBIN HOOD If that's your final decision. I cannot argue with that. I shall be off.

ROBIN HOOD *exits the carriage, jumping smartly out of it with bags in tow.*

MISS SNOB Well hold on...just a minute...not so fast...what about my belongings...what about the bear's head? ...what about...my...

LITTLE JOHN *plonks the* **DRIVER** *back up at the wheel.*

Darren? Darren? Where's Darren? Darren you big fat lazy ogre where...

DARREN *suddenly wakes, startled, like he's fallen asleep on the job.* **ROBIN HOOD** *grabs him by the shoulder...*

ROBIN HOOD Wakey, wakey. Tut tut tut, my my, I do NOT like to be put in this position Darren, I really don't. But as it's the first time I've caught you sleeping at the wheel, I'll let you off...just this once because you're a nice bloke Darren,

I'm feeling generous and I like you, I do. But do it again and I will have to give you a penalty fine.

The **DRIVER** *is shocked, dazed, gawping and nods at* **ROBIN HOOD,** *trying to look awake. Grateful for the free pass.*

MISS SNOB NO! Do NOT give that crook any more money you Giant Mushroom-Bottomed Lump!

ROBIN HOOD Is she always this rude?

DRIVER Pretty much.

ROBIN HOOD Nice cup of coffee should do the trick. Now ride on into Nottingham town my good man...

The **DRIVER** *drives away...*

MISS SNOB NO! NO! Stop! Where's my... STOP the carriage! Darren you Donkey! I've been robbed! HE'S A THIEF! I'VE BEEN ROBBED! HELP! THERE'S BEEN A ROBBERY!

ROBIN HOOD I think you'll find, Miss Snob, that there's actually been a 'SNOBBERY'. Got quite a ring to it really? And besides, we don't say 'ROB', that's such a crass word. We *borrow.* So technically, you've been involved in a 'Borrowry.'

MISS SNOB TELL ME YOUR NAME!

LITTLE JOHN *and* **ROBIN HOOD,** *with their bags of loot, run off into the forest.* **ROBIN** *with his paperwork as proof. Shouting...*

ROBIN HOOD It's a cycle Miss Snob, money goes round and around and around...it's a machine and we are all a part of it, you'll see! What fun! And you were such a great sport. Thanks again!

MISS SNOB TELL ME YOUR NAME! YOU WON'T GET AWAY WITH THIS! I WILL FIND YOU, YOU WRETCHED SNAGGLE-TOOTHED SNAKE! TELL ME YOUR NAME ... I'LL GET YOU, I WILL ... WHO ARE YOU...?

2. Robin Hood

Characters: The **SHERIFF OF NOTTINGHAM, MESSENGER.**

Scene switches super fast to the **SHERIFF OF NOTTINGHAM,** *dressed in his clobber, sitting in his quarters, think Alan Partridge jobsworth deluded loser, surrounded by carafes of purple wine, fruit, weapons and shiny coins. A fire crackles and roars.*

And on the beat he snarls –.

SHERIFF OF NOTTINGHAM Robin Hood.

The **SHERIFF OF NOTTINGHAM** *does not know how to use offensive terms and this is an ongoing annoyance for the* **MESSENGER,** *so throughout the script, when the* **SHERIFF** *tries to 'curse' he is actually making compliments, we see the* **MESSENGER** *react to this with frustration.*

MESSENGER Well, one can't be sure Sheriff...but...it does look like the dirty work of Robin Ho –

SHERIFF OF NOTTINGHAM *Oh WOW! You're so smart, I really hope I get my grades at college so that I can grow up to be a MESSENGER like you!* NOT! Of course it was Robin Hood, it's always Robin Hood! The last thing I need is that *Adorable Little... Bow and Arrowed... Clown* back on my turf, prancing around causing mischief when I'm on such a roll! I want that *Jammy Tart* captured and strung up! FOR GOOD!

MESSENGER Yes Sheriff.

SHERIFF OF NOTTINGHAM NOW!

MESSENGER Oh as in now? I'll just go and see to that then.

Exit **MESSENGER. SHERIFF** *shouts back...*

SHERIFF OF NOTTINGHAM Oh...one more thing... I don't suppose there is an instrument anywhere in the castle?

MESSENGER What, like a weapon Sheriff?

SHERIFF OF NOTTINGHAM No, not 'like a weapon Sheriff' you *Iced Ringed Donut*, or I'D HAVE SAID 'A WEAPON' WOULDN'T I? I want an instrument, something to strum, to keep a rhythm...a guitar, a banjo, a lyre, a harp...a synth?

MESSENGER Oh right. Erm... I don't think we...

SHERIFF OF NOTTINGHAM You have no idea why I'd need that do you? Have you never worked for a villain before or is this your first time?

MESSENGER I... I...

SHERIFF OF NOTTINGHAM Come on you Muppet! Really. *Think.*

MESSENGER Erm...

SHERIFF OF NOTTINGHAM You can't think of why I might need some sort of musical accompaniment at this moment? Absolute amateur, amateurs every time. I'm the villain, so what will they be expecting? Come on...

MESSENGER I... I – honestly, sorry boss, I don't know.

SHERIFF OF NOTTINGHAM They'll be expecting me to sit here now and talk to myself – in monologue form, to begin with, before naturally flowing into a song slash verse.

MESSENGER Right –

SHERIFF OF NOTTINGHAM It's my moment to talk about all my mean and miserable, vile, wretched plans and cunning schemes – talk a bit about what I'm into, flesh it out, make it personal...add those little touches... ALL the villains do it, it's *the* bit. It's a chance for me to show my side of the story but also give them a flavour of me.

MESSENGER What about you Sheriff?

SHERIFF OF NOTTINGHAM Perhaps mention the various trophies I won as a kid, couple of funny anecdotes, my motives as a baddie. Could talk about my siblings, any pets, maybe

mention my first girlfriend. My performance as a keen
golfer – that kind of thing...

MESSENGER Oh yes, you play, what's your handicap?

SHERIFF OF NOTTINGHAM My whatt-i-cap?

MESSENGER Golf? You said you play... I play too, just at
weekends, for fun. What's your handicap?

SHERIFF OF NOTTINGHAM Arrr, well now you're getting personal.
Crossing the lines of professionalism to friendship, eh?
Handi-c...what did you say it was called again?

MESSENGER Handicap, Sheriff.

SHERIFF OF NOTTINGHAM Agh yes, those basic beginners,
golfing terms. We don't really use those words in our
advanced games. So you're taking me back now, bud. Let's
see what can I recall...well of course there's the Cluubbbbbbs
– Gollllfffff Buggies – those triangle diamond patterned
jumpppppperrrrrrsssss? Ah, memories, memories. So...
handicap, for me, *pssshhh*...on a good day, probably reaching
about a solid gold 28?

MESSENGER I'll go and see if we can find you that instrument.

SHERIFF OF NOTTINGHAM Thank you.

MESSENGER I think we have a recorder *knocking* around
somewhere –

SHERIFF OF NOTTINGHAM A record –? What am I, five? I DON'T
WANT A STUPID PRIMARY SCHOOL RECORDER DO I?

MESSENGER I don't know boss.

SHERIFF OF NOTTINGHAM How am I meant to pull off a stunt
like this without a real instrument *You Chocolate Biscuit-
Headed Pretzel*? Embarrassment mate... I can't do that with
a blummin' nasal recorder can I? Meant to be deadly.

MESSENGER I'll see what I can find Sheriff.

SHERIFF OF NOTTINGHAM You do that. Find something good.
Absolute Swan-Feathered Cupcake.

MESSENGER Would you like me to have the recorder bought up to you anyway?

SHERIFF OF NOTTINGHAM NO! I am not going to use a –

MESSENGER – just in case you –

SHERIFF OF NOTTINGHAM – Yes. Yes fine. Bring up the recorder.

MESSENGER *exits.*

Recorder. Stupid. What a *kumquat.*

SHERIFF *gulps back wine. Paces. Begins to talk to himself as he struts about, angrily.*

SO YOU'RE BACK ARE YOU? Robin Hood. ROB. in. DA. HOOD. ROB. BIN. Ha! BIN! Your name has the word bin in it. HA! Bet you didn't think of that did you? Who even calls their child that? It's weird. Your stupid father that's who. And he was just as STUPID as you! And now he's stupid and DEAD! And let me tell you, you've made a BIG mistake coming back to this part of the woods because you'll end up just like HIM. STUPID. Which you already are. And then DEAD! HA!

And stop wearing that hat every day. Bet it stinks.

Yeahhhhh, I'll make you dead alright. So dead. You won't even BELIEVE how DEAD you'll even be.

The **SHERIFF** *stands in the mirror, glares.*

Mu-ha-ha-ha. No, that's not right it's more... MU-HA-HA-HA!

Coughs, splutters, sips wine.

Not as easy as it looks actually that... MU-HA-H- how do they do –

The **MESSENGER** *knocks. The* **SHERIFF** *jumps.*

What NOW?

MESSENGER I've got your rec –

SHERIFF OF NOTTINGHAM OH enter, enter! You scared me.

The **MESSENGER** *bows downs on one knee and presents the* **SHERIFF** *with a recorder. The* **SHERIFF** *is not pleased but snatches the recorder anyway.*

Now get out! *You Surprise Trip to Disneyland*! I need my space.

MESSENGER Yes Sheriff. Good luck with your whole...speech song thing. You go get 'em boss.

The **SHERIFF** *slams the door. The room shudders. The* **SHERIFF** *sits in his chair fiddling with his recorder. Trying to get his fingers around the holes.*

SHERIFF OF NOTTINGHAM *(sings)*
I HAVE ALWAYS FANCIED MYSELF ... AS A FINE MAN ...

He tries to get his notes.

I have always fancied myself... I have always...

He gets frustrated. The **MESSENGER** *barges in.*

MESSENGER One more t –

SHERIFF OF NOTTINGHAM *(sings)*
I HAVE ALWAYS FANCIED MYSELF –

The **SHERIFF** *is startled.*

MESSENGER Ah sorry Sheriff I didn't mean to –

SHERIFF OF NOTTINGHAM FOR THE LOVE OF ... WHAT NOW *YOU MARSHMALLOWED-VOICED ACADEMY AWARD WINNING MOVIE STAR*? You must knock. ALWAYS knock. I could have been... I don't know...flossing my teeth after a spinach smoothie or playing Connect 4 with a really pretty girl or something, you must always –

MESSENGER *begins laughing.*

Why are you laughing?

MESSENGER I'm not.

SHERIFF OF NOTTINGHAM Well you clearly are, why are you laughing? Go on, spit it out.

MESSENGER No, no, it's just... I didn't realise you...you know... *fancied* yourself.

SHERIFF OF NOTTINGHAM Fancied myself – Ohhhh you didn't hear the whole lyric...it's out of context...not fancy like *that*... I don't want to snog myself...it's like...

The SHERIFF *begins to sing...*

[MUSIC NO. 1: "I'VE ALWAYS FANCIED MYSELF"]

I HAVE ALWAYS FANCIED MYSELF AS A FINE MAN.

MESSENGER Ahhh, I see, that makes sense.

SHERIFF OF NOTTINGHAM
RESPECTFUL AND ABIDING BY THE LAW,
BUT MISERY CHANGES A MAN OVER TIME AND
YOU FIND YOURSELF THINKING OF KINDNESS AS A CHORE.

MESSENGER That's good.

SHERIFF OF NOTTINGHAM Oh, is it? OK, I'll keep going then ... ok ... here we go ...
MY MOTHER SAID I WAS ALWAYS A GOOD BOY,
I SAT UP STRAIGHT AND GOBBLED DOWN MY GREENS,
I LEARNT TO SPEAK LATIN AND SHARED MY TOYS
BUT THEN I SMASHED THEM ALL UP IN MY TEENS.

I STARTED WIPING BOGIES UNDER MY BED,
PULLING OFF THE WINGS OF BUTTERFLIES,
I TOOK PLEASURE LEAVING TREASURES ON MY DADS HEAD,
OFTEN IN THE FORM OF A BIG RIPE FART SURPRISE.

THINGS WENT FROM BAD TO WORSE THEN AT THAT POINT,
MY TEACHER SAID I WAS DYSFUNCTIONAL AND BAD,
SO I SNUCK INTO HER HANDBAG AND STOLE A FEW COINS,
AND MY EYEBALLS TURNED A CERTAIN SHADE OF BLACK,

I WAS KICKED OUT OF THAT SCHOOL PRETTY QUICKLY,

MY PARENTS SAID I WAS AN EMBARRASSMENT,
I TRIED TO GET THEIR ATTENTION BY FEIGNING SICKLY
BUT INSTEAD THEY PREFERRED HANGING OUT WITH THIS
  EXCHANGE STUDENT.

The **SHERIFF** *stops playing to explain...*

Now that bit's about...well...at my school there was this
exchange scheme and I took part with a kid from another
school, my exchange student was this girl called Monica from
Poland. Very strange girl. Ate whole mozzarella balls like
apples. Actual *Apples*. Liked origami. Odd. And Mum and
Dad, they just took a real shining to the girl. Everything was
just *Monica this, Monica that,* no NOT Monica ANYTHING.

MESSENGER Right. That sounds...difficult.

SHERIFF OF NOTTINGHAM Never got the chance to go to Poland
did I? Not a very fair exchange if you ask me. That was
when I realised that life isn't fair, life is like a backstabbing
exchange student that comes to England and kidnaps your
parents' affection and eats all your Coco Pops and before
you know it, is given your bedroom and you're in the small
box room with the exercise bike and clothes horse. That,
Monica, is not a fair exchange. Just like life isn't.

The **SHERIFF** *gets teary. Inhales. Exhales.*

I GOT A SUMMER JOB AT A CAR WASH,
VERGING ON DEPRESSION ON ALL THE TIME
I ALSO WAS QUITE GANGLY WITH A FEW SPOTS
AND WAS TEASED BY THE MEAN KIDS ALL THE TIME

– I don't like this song anymore.

The **SHERIFF** *gets very emotional.*

It's stupid. I don't like it. It's pointless. It's not how it's
meant to sound... I –

MESSENGER No, honestly, Sheriff, it's really good, I really like
it, I –

SHERIFF OF NOTTINGHAM SHUT UP! IT'S NOT! This is not about me it's about that Button Nosed Robin Hood.

Went completely off piste. Nobody wants to hear about all of that –

MESSENGER I do, you were right, it *is* nice to get to know a bit more about you, Sheriff, you're such an enigma of a man –

SHERIFF OF NOTTINGHAM STOP IT! NO! NOW GO! Leave me to be with my thoughts you *Leisurely Walk In The Park!* Now, let me get on to my real song.

MESSENGER Oh, can't I watch?

SHERIFF OF NOTTINGHAM NO! YOU CAN'T YOU *WARM BUBBLE BATH.* JUST GET OUT. GET OUT!

MESSENGER Very well Sheriff.

The SHERIFF *shuts the* MESSENGER *out. The atmosphere deepens and darkens, almost to like a Nick Cave/Tom Waits moment. The* SHERIFF *is seething.*

[MUSIC NO. 2: "ROBIN HOOD"]

ROBIN HOOD. ROBIN HOOD.
THE MOST WANTED NAME IN THE BIG BAD WOODS,
I WANT YOU CAPTURED, UNDERSTOOD?
AND YOUR ASHES BURNT INTO FISH FOOD!
SO WHERE ARE YOU? ROBIN HOOD?
I'LL HANG YOU A ROPE TO WEAR WITH THAT HOOD,
I HATE YOUR FACE, THAT GHASTLY LOOK,
YOU'RE A SHAMED DISGRACE, A FRAUD, A CROOK,
'OH I'M GOODY GOODY ROBIN HOOD,
SO KIND AND NICE AND MISUNDERSTOOD,
I TAKE FROM THE BAD TO GIVE TO THE GOOD.'
IT'S CALLED STEALING MATE AND IT'S VERY ... RUDE!
ROBIN HOOD YOU'RE TOO BIG FOR YOUR BOOTS,
RUNNING ROUND TOWN LIKE YOU OWN THE HOOD.
WELL YOU'LL BE BURIED DEEP DOWN WITH THE TREE'S
   ROOTS SOON,

COS THERE'S A PRICE ON YOUR HEAD AND I'M COMING FOR
   YOU...
SO I'D RUN, RUN ROBIN HOOD...IF I WERE YOU...

Recorder solo. The **SHERIFF** *gets really really into it.*

That's actually not bad.

He plays some more...

ROBIN HOOD. ROBIN HOOD.
THE MOST WANTED NAME IN THE BIG BAD WOODS,
I WANT YOU CAPTURED, UNDERSTOOD?
AND YOUR ASHES BURNT INTO FISH FOOD!
SO I'D RUN, RUN ROBIN HOOD...IF I WERE YOU...

The **SHERIFF** *spits, snarling, throwing darts at the
reward poster with* **ROBIN**'s *smiling face on it.*

Like somewhere really far...like I dunno...maybe the moon...

The **SHERIFF** *holds his deadly pose, eyes slitting, looking
out deadly to the audience, sucking his cheekbones in.*

Or something.

3. The Real Robin

Characters: **ROBIN HOOD, LITTLE JOHN, ALAN, SCARLET, MERRY MEN X2.**

The woods in a new morning light, hazing orange, pink, brown leaves. Globes of tear drop dew hang on the end of blades of grass. The sound of nature waking up for the day; a trickling silver stream.

ROBIN HOOD *and* **LITTLE JOHN,** *breathless, appear in this new neck of the woods, throwing down their bags of loot, trying to get their breaths back.* **ROBIN** *rips off the fake moustache and* **LITTLE JOHN** *unpeels his own disguise. Although tired, the pair do their rehearsed celebratory ritual of a handshake – elbow to elbow – bum to bum – shove-hand clap – fist bump routine. And* **LITTLE JOHN** *collapses at the base of a tree where* **ROBIN**'s *wanted mugshot is nailed, he's exhausted and begins to snack on the riches.* **ROBIN** *takes jacket off, leans by the stream, washes face and then removes hat, suddenly reels of beautiful rolling hair tumble out from the hat. And it is becomes clear –* **ROBIN** *is a girl.*

She splashes water on her face and drinks. Passes a beaker of water to **LITTLE JOHN.**

LITTLE JOHN Thanks mate. Horrible woman weren't she?

ROBIN HOOD Ha! I quite liked her, in that way one can become oddly fascinated with horrible women. Thought she was gonna chop your head off at one point though!

LITTLE JOHN Me too! Could you imagine, I mean, who would want me on their dining room wall?

LITTLE JOHN *does an impression.*

ROBIN HOOD Hahaha no thanks, Little John, that'd put me right off my chicken dinner.

LITTLE JOHN Ahhh, this is the life...

ROBIN HOOD Nearly, more work to do for now but one day. One day we can sleep and sleep and sleep.

LITTLE JOHN Let's just hope it's not in a grave or prison cell.

ROBIN HOOD Nah, they won't catch us.

> **ROBIN** *stares out into the distance, gazing at the stream, the sun. A little* **BUSY BODY** *of a man stumbles by in an authoritative fashion, paying no attention to the pair as he stuffily struts past and smacks an even higher reward price on* **ROBIN***'s wanted poster.* **ROBIN** *is standing in the exact same pose as her poster portrays her.*

BUSY BODY Good day.

> *He huffs off in his pompous little march leaving* **LITTLE JOHN** *and* **ROBIN** *confused.*

LITTLE JOHN/ROBIN HOOD Good day...?

> **LITTLE JOHN** *considers the Wanted Poster.*

LITTLE JOHN Jeeeeeezzzzzz! How much? I might go ahead and turn you in *myself* for a price like that!

ROBIN HOOD Ha! You should! And split the winnings with me!

LITTLE JOHN I don't get why you're 'wanted.' You're not exactly something I would put on my letter to Father Christmas, don't they know how difficult you are? They could have you for free.

ROBIN HOOD No that Sheriff isn't getting *me* for free. No chance. He got my Dad for free. And he was worth a million of me. No, if he wants me dead, he's going to have to pay, Little John.

LITTLE JOHN Well just so he knows, if he *does* want to buy you off me, I'll accept cash or sweetcorn also, sweetcorn is probably my favourite alternative to money.

ROBIN HOOD Shall I call the others?

LITTLE JOHN Can't we just take one little small tincy tiny nap first?

> **LITTLE JOHN** *puts* **ROBIN**'s *hat over his eyes and hands* **ROBIN** *her bow. She plucks an arrow and strikes the arrow up and into the sky, it makes a bird like cry, soaring through the air and slicing down. Within moments The* **MERRY MANY** *arrive including* **WILL SCARLET** *and* **ALAN-A-DALE**. *Knowing they are safe they take over the scene, flying down from the dizzy lofty heights of the trees, colouring the stage in with a confident sense of play, entitlement and ownership. Climbing down trees, abseiling down the canopies of green, clambering through bushes, scampering down rope, almost appearing out of the trees and woods like camouflaged acrobatic moths. Their home, built into nature, reveals itself. Bunks, huts, a make-shift watermill, a log fire. All the while, cheering, chinking and swigging their home-made boozy brews, acting up and making* **LITTLE JOHN** *and* **ROBIN HOOD** *giggle.*

[MUSIC NO. 3: "OUTLAWS"]

MERRY MANY
OH WE'RE OUTLAWS,
WANTED FOR,
WHAT WE SAID OR DONE
WE RUN TOGETHER, ROLL TOGETHER,
LIVING ON THE RUN,
THE SHERIFF PLUCKED OUT A PRICE AND STUCK IT ON OUR
    HEADS,
HE WON'T GIVE UP THE HUNT FOR US UNTIL HE HAS US
    DEAD.

OH WE'RE OUTLAWS,
FIGHTING FOR,
JUSTICE NOT REVENGE,
OUT IN THE WOODS BUT IT'S ALL GOOD,

COS FREEDOM DON'T CHARGE RENT.

SOME SAY WE'RE FERAL THAT THE DEVIL WON'T FORGET OUR
NAMES,

BUT WE GOT A BARRELS FILLED WITH ALE

ALAN-A-DALE

WE'RE TOO DRUNK TO COMPLAIN!

MERRY MANY

OH WE'RE OUTLAWS,

STINKING POOR

BUT RICH IN OUR OWN WAY,

HAPPY AS KINGS, WE LAUGH AND SING,

AND TAXES WE WON'T PAY,

COS TAXES ARE JUST AXES AND THE BLADES AIM FOR OUR
THROATS

A MERRY MANY

(FEMALE?) BUT FOR A BUNCH OF CRIMINALS YOU WON'T
MEET NICER BLOKES.

MERRY MEN

OH WE'RE OUTLAWS,

WITH NO FRONT DOORS,

BUT OUR DAYS ARE HAPPIER,

WE FILL OUR CUPS WITH LOVELY STUFF,

COS IT MAKES US MERRIER,

WE GOT THE STRENGTH TO FIGHT BACK FOR OUR FAIR SHARE
OF THE PIE,

NO CLASS DIVIDE COULD SPLIT OUR SIDE COS WE'LL JUST
MULTIPLY

A MERRY MANY

TOO RIGHT!

LITTLE JOHN

AND NO OUTLAW,

DO WE LOVE MORE,

THAN OUR GIRL ROBIN HOOD,

SOME SAY SHE'S POSH, LOADED WITH DOSH,

BUT SHE'S MISUNDERSTOOD,

SHE'D RISK HER LIFE FOR LOYALTY, HOLDS US UP BRICK BY
    BRICK,
BUT STILL GOT THE NERVE TO BOSS US ROUND

ALAN-A-DALE
(VERY DRUNK IN A DEEP VOICE) ...COS OUR BOSS IS A CHICK!

> **ALAN** *burps. Other* **MERRY MANY** *look nervous at the
> 'chick' bomb.* **ROBIN** *rolls her eyes. Song repeats as the*
> **MANY** *hunker down until settled.* **ROBIN** *talks to the
> audience as though they are also the* **MERRY MANY.**

ROBIN HOOD My Merry Many. First thing on today's agenda,
same as yesterday and the day before it seems. Tedious, but
it bares repeating: How Not To Be A Complete and Utter
Moron, chapter one.

ALAN-A-DALE I don't remember doing that yesterday.

ROBIN HOOD Funny that, because it does seem to be suspiciously
missing from your repertoire.

A MERRY MANY Can't you give us the crash course?

ROBIN HOOD Firstly I am not your *boss*. We have NO bosses
out here, we are, as you so beautifully-*ish* sung, outlaws.
Estranged from our town, people and families, with prices
on our heads, some of us with more attractive hefty prices
than others, dare I say it, but prices none the less. But I
assure you that we are equal. Outlaw next to outlaw. Men
and women alike.

LITTLE JOHN We're just like baked beans.

ROBIN HOOD How John, are we like baked beans?

LITTLE JOHN They may try and label us differently on the
shelf, like we're different brands, make some tins look more
expensive than others because of the packaging or what
not, but really, we are all...just baked beans.

ROBIN HOOD Very good Little John.

LITTLE JOHN Little baked beans...swimming around in their beany bean juice.

ROBIN HOOD Less of the 'juice' please but yes –

LITTLE JOHN You could dress up your beans even, add a little paprika, serve alongside a gourmet fish pie or just eat cold out the tin, still, baked beans though. Equal. Hearty. Wholesome and deli –

ROBIN HOOD Are you working for baked beans or something now?

LITTLE JOHN No, I'm currently unemployed actually. But if anybody wants any odd jobs doing, painting, grouting, I'm not a plumber per se, but I've fixed a couple of bogs in my ti –

ROBIN HOOD The mission was executed as planned and thankfully nobody was hurt in the process –

LITTLE JOHN Not completely true, I did actually get a whitlow during the experience, Robin, but I didn't like to make a fuss at the time.

ALAN-A-DALE What's a whitlow then?

LITTLE JOHN Oh. Thank you for asking Alan-a-Dale, it's basically a minor abscess near the soft tissue of the fingernail. It's not a *major* big deal. Just can be a pain when I say like... eat a satsuma for example. Citrus. Acid. It burns.

A MERRY MANY I know the ones. Hate that.

ROBIN HOOD Oh poor you Little John. We'll be sure to take you to hospital to get that seen to.

LITTLE JOHN Oh no, it's not an emergency, honestly there's no need to go –

ROBIN HOOD No, no, I insist, I really think we should risk our lives and make the trip into town and rush you into A&E with all the other victims of whitlows, stubbed toes and papercuts.

LITTLE JOHN Ha! You don't go to A&E for a *papercut*, Robin, you just – Oh, you're being sarcastic...

ROBIN HOOD Guys. The mission was executed as planned but sadly...aborted. We come back to Sherwood pretty much empty handed.

The **MERRY MANY** *look disappointed. Groaning.*

The driver of the carriage was far too strong for us and the passenger was far too...

LITTLE JOHN Annoying.

ROBIN HOOD Annoying yes. Very annoying. We tried our very best, put up a good fight, but there was no point risking the revealing of our identities.

MERRY MANY *grumble.*

A MERRY MANY Understandable, sometimes a borrowy just isn't worth the risk.

ALAN-A-DALE Glad you made it back in one piece. That's all that's important.

ROBIN HOOD Thank you. We are pleased to be back.

ALAN-A-DALE There's plenty of food still, we can stretch the grains and the milk is a bit off but that's basically how you make cheese anyway if you don't mind spreading it onto a cracker made out of bark and holding your nose.

A MERRY MAN Actually very tasty.

ROBIN HOOD Ahh, good, you're always so high in spirits. I think that sounds like a very humble yet fulfilling meal but perhaps best to save that for desperate measures...besides we will need to conserve our energy for EATING ALL OF THIS LUX GRUB!

ROBIN HOOD *and* **LITTLE JOHN** *reveal big bags stuffed with stolen edible goodies. Bread, wine, cheese, pies, cakes, fruit, meat, grapes. The* **MERRY MANY** *cheer.*

Tonight we shall feast!

This is the start of our wonderful futures, we've been under a grey sky but soon that sky will lift and we shall have back our liberty and power, stick with me and I promise we will see golden days. But before we gorge ourselves to sleep we must do our bit.

ALAN-A-DALE Aghhh, we're all starving! Can we just get on and eat?

ROBIN HOOD After, Alan. The sheriff is coming to collect his greedy taxes and our people will be relying on us to share the wealth that we've rightfully retrieved to pay him off.

WILL SCARLET Oh *what*?

ROBIN HOOD Oh what *what* Will Scarlet?

WILL SCARLET 'Our people.' Yeah, alright.

ROBIN HOOD I beg your pardon, is there something you'd like to say?

WILL SCARLET It's just...no...forget it...

ROBIN HOOD Oh no, please go on, your opinions are never wasted on me.

WILL SCARLET It's just... I don't get why we have to *share* it? Those people aren't the ones living out here in the woods like animals, are they? It's us! Why should they get our earnings?

A MERRY MANY We got family out there mate! My kids are out there –

ALAN-A-DALE And mine.

LITTLE JOHN My old dear.

ROBIN HOOD And soon you shall all be able to go home and live with them. But for now we have to give them what we can before the Sheriff starves them to death!

WILL SCARLET Well I don't even have anybody there so what difference does that make to me? I don't have a home to go back to.

ROBIN HOOD Well let us be your home.

WILL SCARLET Ha, this isn't a home. I don't get why we put our lives in danger for strangers. Why share?

The **MERRY MANY** *groan at* **WILL.**

ROBIN HOOD Are you not hungry Will Scarlet?

WILL SCARLET Yeah, course.

ROBIN HOOD So should I not *share* this food and wine with you?

WILL SCARLET It's different.

ROBIN HOOD How? You *need* to eat don't you? Can't live on berries and rabbit ears forever.

WILL, *ashamed, shrugs.*

Just I don't remember seeing you when we borrowed our takings, that doesn't mean I don't trust that you aren't doing your bit to contribute. We all play our part, Will Scarlet.

WILL SCARLET *looks annoyed. The* **MERRY MANY** *look down.*

RIGHT! There seems to be some confusion in our camp. Let me clarify. As it appears some of us here need reminding... Our home has been confiscated by a tyrant. Since King Richard the Lionheart has left for his crusade we are under the thumb, lock and key of a merciless and barbaric man. The Sheriff has no empathy and there's no reasoning with him. Please do not EVER think for a second that living in the extremities of today's ruthless tax and penalty charges that there is wiggle room for selfishness. Forget what you had before. Because that is not life outside of these woods anymore.

We live for now! We are The Merry Many and we fight for now! We can help! We are young, fit and able.

ALAN-A-DALE And wanted! Ha!

ROBIN HOOD And yes, wanted. We are wanted but there is freedom in that too. I mean, we're already in deep trouble – how much deeper can we get? We can help those the same way we would like to help ourselves and each other. We take from those that have enough to spare, we share and we reward ourselves for our hard work with food and wine and the company of our friends. The things that money can't buy.

MERRY MANY *cheer.*

LITTLE JOHN And besides *we* don't pay tax in the forest. Money is worthless to us out here.

WILL SCARLET If we're the ones living out here like this then we at least *deserve* to enjoy the perks.

ROBIN HOOD Deserve? What does anyone *deserve?* We have silver service, luxury accommodation. The forest pays *us*, richly, beautifully, with the golden warmth of the smiling orange sun every morning, the clean clear fresh spring of the stream that washes us, our skin, our clothes and quenches our thirst. The way the trees and bushes provide us with shelter, beds, places to hide, to keep safe. The fruits from branches that are sweet and ripe that you can pluck from your bedside. The ground gives us wheat. Corn. The air is ours, the harmony of birdsong that lullabies us to sleep, the pearl torch of a moon that protects us each and every night. That keeps us sound. Fearless. Brave. This forest gives us everything.

The **MERRY MANY** *cheer in agreement.*

And if you don't like that, Will, you don't have to stick with us. You can go back to town where your hands will be tied and you'll be captured and strung up. Gutted. Then, you'll see how much you think you *deserve.*

LITTLE JOHN You didn't even do the work. We did.

ROBIN HOOD We all play our parts John, allow the others to play theirs. Will, you in?

WILL SCARLET Not only do we not see the takings, you're then asking us to risk our lives to give to these people. If the Sheriff catches us handing out money, *stolen* money, it's game over for us.

ROBIN HOOD I am sure the people of Nottingham are very grateful to you, Will Scarlet, you are doing something meaningful, something good. It will not go unnoticed. It will not be forgotten. I swear it.

ALAN-A-DALE But Scarlet is right, I get all the handing out, course, but there must be better, safer ways of smuggling, so we don't get caught?

The **MERRY MANY** *agree.*

ROBIN HOOD I hear you. This will be our last time this way. I will keep you safe until then, I promise. Scarlet?

ROBIN *holds her hand out to* **WILL SCARLET. SCARLET** *is reluctant but stands and shakes* **ROBIN**'s *hand.* **WILL** *looks to* **LITTLE JOHN** *as though he's the traitor.*

LITTLE JOHN Grab a bag.

[MUSIC NO. 4: "TAKE THESE COINS"]

ROBIN HOOD TAKE THESE COINS AND SHARE THEM OUT,
BE FAIR AND GENEROUS WITH YOURSELVES,
FOR THERE IS PLENTY TO GO ROUND,
SO HELP ANOTHER TO HELP YOURSELF.

ROBIN *hands out chocolate gold coins to* **MERRY MANY** *who throw them out to audience.*

THIS TOWN IS STEALING FROM ITSELF,
THIEVING FROM ITS BITTER HELL,
STARVING IN ITS BLOCKED OUT CELL,
SINCE BRAVE LIONHEART LEFT WITH HIS BELT.
WHILST THE GOOD KING IS AWAY,

THE SHERIFF CLASSES THE POOR AS STRAYS,
AS WAIFS THEY FRAY AS TIME DECAYS,
THERE'S A CLOUD OVER OUR TOWN AND IT'S GREY.
HE'LL TAKE THE AIR, THE GRASS, THE FLOWERS,
BINGE ON ANY SOURCE OF POWER,
AND WATCH ON FROM HIS SHERIFF TOWER,
WHILST MOTHER'S MILK STILL CURDLES SOUR.

YOUR CLUTCH OF GRAINS IS NOW HIS LAND,
HIS CASTLE BUILT FROM YOUR SCOOPED SAND,
HE COUNTS THE GOLD YOU DUG AND PANNED,
AND TAXES SNATCHED IN HIS COLD HANDS.

HE WON'T KNOW WHAT IT'S LIKE NOT TO EAT,
TO FEEL THE MUD BENEATH YOUR FEET,
OR THE KISS OF DEATH PLANTING YOUR CHEEKS,
OR MEET MAGGOT MEN THAT CHEW YOUR WHEAT.

HE WON'T KNOW HOW IT HURTS TO BE WEAK,
WHEN YOUR FAMILY GO WITHOUT A FEED,
HE CUTS YOU DOWN LIKE YOU'RE YELLOW WEEDS,
AND STEALS YOUR SUGAR FOR HIS TEA.

WHILST THE MEEK MILD PRINCE PLAYS KING,
THE SHERIFF IS OUT COLLECTING,
STOLEN COINS IN HIS ROTTEN TIN,
THAT'LL NEVER PAY FOR HIS GREEDY SINS.

BUT WE, THE OUTLAWS, LIVE IN THE WILD,
AS BROTHER, SISTER, PARENT, CHILD,
FIGHTING CRIMINALS WITH THEIR OWN CRIMES,
WITH REMORSE FOR THE POOR FOR EVERY RICH DOOR'S
    DIME.

SO TAKE THESE COINS AND SHARE THEM OUT,
BE FAIR AND GENEROUS WITH YOURSELVES,
NO NEED TO BEG, NO NEED TO SCROUNGE...
WHEN YOU HELP ANOTHER TO HELP YOURSELF.

MANY *cheer and hand out coins. Chinking their bottles.*
Except for WILL, *he dumps the bags down.*

WILL SCARLET It's easy for you to say Robin. But you don't
know what that's like either. You have more in common with
that money grabbing sheriff than you do us. You come from
money. From a stinkin' rich father. You grew up in some
posh castle. We didn't.

LITTLE JOHN Hey! Oi, Scarlet! Enough!

WILL SCARLET You're just a goody-goody privileged princess
toff with a smart mouth that's got herself in a little bit
too much trouble and is just out here having a bit of fun,
biding her time, bossing us lot around giving it the big'un,
enjoying herself until she gets bored, when she's had enough
of living in the wild like us and she hasn't got all of her girly
luxuries. Until she decides she doesn't like the make-believe
fairy tale game of pretending she's *poor* anymore. One day
you'll decide you're sick of being 'one of us MERRY Many'
and decide to run back home and cry to daddy.

LITTLE JOHN *steps forward to* WILL, *protective over*
ROBIN.

ROBIN HOOD John, don't – leave it.

WILL SCARLET Yeah, don't worry John, I'm not going to hurt
your little spoilt girlfriend.

The MERRY MANY *look sheepish.*

ROBIN HOOD Yes my father had money. He worked hard for
it. He was respected. He was a good man. And that Sheriff,
that *you* compare me to, murdered him. And you should be
grateful that I am nothing like him because then I might
just do something stupid like I don't know, maybe murder
you too. But luckily, for you, I'm not. Instead, I offer you
what I have. Eat with us, drink with us, share the coins
with your neighbours.

WILL *takes the bags.*

Maybe it upsets you, Will, that I'm a woman? That I'm *providing*? But that's your problem not mine, Scarlet.

MERRY MANY *take bags, disburse, unpacking the loot.* **ROBIN** *ups and goes in different direction.*

LITTLE JOHN Robin? Where you going?

ROBIN HOOD To see an old friend.

LITTLE JOHN Want me to come along for the journey?

ROBIN HOOD No, you stay. Rest. Just going to try my luck, make the most of my time as a free woman.

LITTLE JOHN Ahh, kind of like a bucket list type thing before the sheriff turns you into brown bread?

ROBIN HOOD Huh?

LITTLE JOHN Brown bread...it means dead.

ROBIN HOOD Little John, your cockney rhyming slang vocab is wasted on me.

LITTLE JOHN They're right you know Robin. We are clever with the taking, we gotta be clever with the giving too. We don't want to get locked up for doing a good thing.

ROBIN HOOD I know John, I'm working on it.

LITTLE JOHN Something up your sleeve, I won't ask questions but I assume it's to do with your 'old friend.' She hates you, you know.

ROBIN HOOD Who does?

LITTLE JOHN Maid Marion.

ROBIN HOOD No she doesn't.

LITTLE JOHN O...k...all I'm saying is, good luck.

ROBIN HOOD You keep your luck John for yourself, share it out with the others.

LITTLE JOHN Haha. Be safe Robin.

ROBIN HOOD Brown Bread. Dead. They don't all work, but that, yes, that one, I like it. I do.

Exit **ROBIN**. **LITTLE JOHN** *waves her off and lies down for a rest.* **WILL SCARLET** *sticks around to watch* **ROBIN** *leave.*

WILL SCARLET Where's she off to then, eh?

LITTLE JOHN To see some old friend from school, Marion.

WILL SCARLET Oh great, I get it, so pack us off to do the dirty work whilst she swans off to have a girl's brunch, meanwhile...you kip on the job.

LITTLE JOHN Will, to get that stuff there, I had to be hit by a carriage, knock out a man, carry a ton of steals back through the woods and worst of all, *run*. I think I'm allowed a little rest.

WILL SCARLET I don't get it John, why should we have to listen to everything *she* says?

LITTLE JOHN Because we are terrified of her, REMEMBER?

LITTLE JOHN, *jokes, sits up.*

Because she knows what's best for us, she cares about us. Robin's a good person Will, I know you don't see it but you have to trust her. I do and I'm a better man for it.

LITTLE JOHN *lies back down and* **WILL** *takes his bags and follows after the others.*

4. Friar Tuck

Characters: **ROBIN HOOD, FRIAR TUCK.**

ROBIN *is thrashing through the woods cutting down brambles and wheat, tearing her way through the off beaten track. She is singing to herself, content. She settles down at the stream, stopping for a drink. She considers how she's going to cross the stream. She is being watched. She senses it. She turns with her bow and arrow.*

ROBIN HOOD Show yourself to me.

ROBIN *angles her arrow, razor sharp, swivelling quick. The atmosphere transforms, becomes creepy, dark and eerie. Unsettling. Shadows and foreboding sense of unease. Crows caw.* **ROBIN** *is alone.*

I am armed. With an arrow. And a bow. And I am bloody good at using it too.

Rustling. The air is stiff with tension. **ROBIN** *shoots an arrow blindly into the long grass.*

FRIAR TUCK OWWWWWW!

ROBIN *tramples over.*

ROBIN HOOD Who are you and why are you spying on me?

FRIAR TUCK Spying on you? I'm not spying on you. I was... *bird* watching.

ROBIN *is not impressed.*

Until you shot me. In the bum.

ROBIN HOOD Well I want my arrow back.

FRIAR TUCK It's in my bum cheek now. A part of my bum. Not yours. SO technically it belongs to me.

ROBIN HOOD Give me back my arrow or I shall shoot you in the other bum cheek so all your farts shall forever come out in stripes.

FRIAR TUCK Ahhhh ok, ok, ok…

ROBIN *plucks out her arrow, the* **FRIAR** *yelps.*

ROBIN HOOD What are you drinking?

FRIAR TUCK Ribena?

ROBIN HOOD Give it here.

ROBIN *snatches the bottle and has a big glug.*

That's excellent Ribena. I want to cross the stream.

FRIAR TUCK So cross it.

ROBIN HOOD No, I don't think you understand. I want you to carry me.

FRIAR TUCK Why should I carry you?

ROBIN HOOD Because A. I don't want to ruin my best boots and turn up to see my friend soaking wet and B. I just spared your bum's life you so owe me a favour.

FRIAR TUCK What if I don't?

ROBIN HOOD I guess I'll have to think of other places to shoot you.

FRIAR TUCK Up you get then.

ROBIN *climbs onto the* **FRIAR***'s back.*

ROBIN HOOD Giddy-up! There we go, see? This can be your good deed for the day.

They enter the water.

FRIAR TUCK YAAOOOWWW! It's freezing!

ROBIN HOOD Stop being a baby!

FRIAR TUCK There's still time to swim you know…

ROBIN *puts on a cheesy American reporter voice.*

ROBIN HOOD Citizens have been flummoxed throughout the globe after reported sightings of a strange bald-headed beast sporting a poo brown potato sack of a nightdress –

FRIAR TUCK Poo? It's not poo! And it's not a DRESS! Why does everybody call it a dress?

ROBIN HOOD – Wading through water, Mrs Baker said she was just 'Minding my own business out picking dandelions when out of nowhere I stumbled across what can only be the strangest darn thing I ever did see gliding through the water...it was almost like a boat...but not quite...a wooden one because he was wearing so much of that poo brown colour...'

FRIAR TUCK Stop with this poo colour, it's not 'poo.'

ROBIN HOOD Sorry, what colour would you say it was?

FRIAR TUCK I don't know...cappucino? Mocha maybe?

ROBIN HOOD *Mocha.* Please. Don't fool yourself. It's poo.

FRIAR TUCK I don't need this, I don't owe you any –

ROBIN *digs her arrow into the* FRIAR's *neck.*

ROBIN HOOD ... 'but on closer inspection I realised that it, the thing, was moving at the pace of an animal... I mean, I thought I, ME, Mrs Baker, was witnessing the real life legend of Big Foot!'

FRIAR TUCK What are you on about?

ROBIN *then changes voice to an old school circus ring master voice...*

ROBIN HOOD Is it a bird? Noooooo!!

FRIAR TUCK Huh?

ROBIN HOOD Is it a plane? Nooooo!!

FRIAR TUCK Is what a plane?

ROBIN HOOD NO! Ladies and gentleman, boys and girls, grannies and granddads and mums and dads and aunts and uncles and godparents and step-parents and guardians and hamster Colin at home spinning around on his little wheel thing introducing the first ever, one and only... HUMAN FERRY!

FRIAR TUCK No, no, no, that's enough.

[MUSIC NO. 5: "HUMAN BEING FERRY"]

ROBIN HOOD

IF THERE'S A LAKE YOU WANNA CROSS,
WITH NO WAY OF GETTING YOU THERE,
NO STEPPING STONES TO HELP YOU ALONG,
NO PADDLE OR INFLATABLE CHAIR.

FRIAR TUCK No, I know where this is going and I don't like it.

ROBIN HOOD

IF THERE'S A PATCH OF GREEN TO SEE,
BUT YOU JUST DON'T HAVE A BOAT,
NO SURF BOARD OR CANOE, NO, NO,
AND YOU'LL GET WET IF YOU FLOAT.

THEN LOOK NO FURTHER,
THOSE DAYS ARE OVER,
AS ADVERTISED ON THE TELLY,
HE'S AS BIG AS BOULDER,

WRAP YOUR ARMS ROUND THE SHOULDERS –
OF THE HUMAN BEING FERRY!

FRIAR TUCK NO, I don't like this song!

ROBIN HOOD

IF THERE'S A LOVELY COOL CAFE,
JUST THE OTHER SIDE OF THE STREAM,
BUT WITH NO ROW BOAT FOR YOU IN TOW,
YOUR LIFE IS DISTANT FROM A DREAM.

SOME DAYS YOU WISH YOU WERE A FISH,

TO SPLISH SPLASH YOURSELF WITH THE WAVES,
BUT YOU'RE AN AVERAGE KID THAT STILL CAN'T SWIM,
TOO BAD YOU WEREN'T BORN A MERMAID.

FRIAR TUCK A mermaid – honestly? This is just ridiculous.

ROBIN HOOD
BUT LOOK NO FURTHER,
THOSE DAYS WERE NUMBERED,
WRAP YOUR LEGS ROUND HIS BELLY,
LOW COST, LOW EMISSION,
AND ENERGY EFFICIENT,
THE HUMAN BEING FERRY

FRIAR TUCK I will drop you right here in this freezing water if you carry on!

ROBIN HOOD
IT'S BORING TRAVELLING ON YOUR OWN,
WELL HERE'S TRANSPORT WITH CONVERSATION,
IF HE'S GRUMPY TO START, JUST A SHOT OF A DART,
IS ALL IT TAKES FOR SOME PERSUASION.

FRIAR TUCK Grumpy? How is this grumpy?

ROBIN HOOD
COME RAIN, WIND, HAIL, SHINE OR SNOW,
THE HUMAN FERRY IS ALWAYS IN TOWN,
SO LONG AS YOU DON'T MIND THE FACT HE'S SO SLOW,
OR THE COLOUR OF POO BROWN.

FRIAR TUCK Right. That's it, I've had it up to here with you... you can get off my back.

ROBIN HOOD Wouldn't you like to maybe sing a bit Friar?

FRIAR TUCK NO, I do NOT!

ROBIN HOOD Whhaaat? Are you sure? I think the additional live music element gives a real charm to the ferrying experience...

ROBIN *threatens the* **FRIAR** *by putting an arrow to his neck.*

Don't you?

FRIAR TUCK *bursts into song and is actually brilliant.*

FRIAR TUCK
>WELL LOOK NO FURTHER,
>TITANIC MOVE OVER,
>JUST TOP HIS ENGINE UP WITH SHERRY,
>TO GET TO YOUR DESTINATION.
>IN MANS OWN INVENTION,
>THE HUMAN BEING FERRY!

ROBIN HOOD THE HUMAN BEING FERRY! Alright!

FRIAR TUCK THE HUMAN BEING FERRY!

ROBIN HOOD COME ON!

FRIAR TUCK/ROBIN HOOD THE HUMAN BEING FERRYY YYYYY!!!!

The pair battle for the last note and then the **FRIAR** *puts* **ROBIN** *down on the other side of the stream and suddenly switches on* **ROBIN**. *Holding out his sword.*

ROBIN HOOD But we just made music together! How could you?

FRIAR TUCK Think I don't know who you are? I've seen your little 'wanted' posters you know.

ROBIN HOOD Oh *those things*.

FRIAR TUCK You're a criminal.

ROBIN HOOD All press is good press but don't believe *everything* you hear.

FRIAR TUCK I should turn you in.

ROBIN HOOD What, for the reward? Broke are you?

FRIAR TUCK No, because it's the right thing to do.

ROBIN HOOD And sacking off work to creep into the woods to sleep in the sun with your special *Ribena* on The Lord's Day is also the RIGHT thing to be doing, is it?

FRIAR TUCK I just come here for a moments peace, to think, to escape for a bit.

ROBIN HOOD Good for you. I know what it's like in town, I've come back to find misery and poverty on every door step of Nottingham, it's no place to live, it's not a community, it's not a home. I can see why you want to escape. I do good work.

FRIAR TUCK That doesn't mean that the 'good work' you do isn't breaking the law. It's the wrong way to go about it. It's illegal. No matter the motive intended it's still criminal action.

ROBIN HOOD Gross. Have you heard yourself?

FRIAR TUCK Robin Hood, I hearby sentence you to Citizens Arrest, you do not have to say anything but anything you do say may...harm...no...anything you say or do...might... Oh, I don't know the dratted words, I've never arrested anybody before, have I?

ROBIN HOOD Well I count myself as your first then.

FRIAR TUCK Yes and it's a good one. Capturing the most Wanted Woman in England is not a bad start at all.

ROBIN HOOD Ah but you'll have to capture her first.

> **ROBIN** *takes out her sword. The pair sword fight. The* **FRIAR** *is a top sword fighter and knocks* **ROBIN**'s *sword out of her hand, clanging it to the ground.* **ROBIN** *tries to reach for her bow but the* **FRIAR** *is too quick, holding the tip of his blade under* **ROBIN**'s *throat.*

Wait...please...what's your name?

> *The* **FRIAR** *holds his sword.*

FRIAR TUCK Friar Tuck.

ROBIN HOOD Well, Friar Tuck... I have just one question...

FRIAR TUCK Go on...

ROBIN HOOD Did we just become best friends?

5. Tax Day

Characters: **SHERIFF, MESSENGER, WILL SCARLET, ALAN,** (**GUARD**).

Nottingham. Under a grey cloud. The town is full of tension and apprehension for it is Tax Day. When the mean and merciless **SHERIFF** *comes round to collect taxes from the people of Nottingham. We see mayhem, chaos and fear as the locals scramble together to meet the* **SHERIFF'S** *impossible demands.*

A clanging death bell rings. The **SHERIFF** *appears, strong and mighty (in his head) with a whistle and a megaphone. The* **SHERIFF** *addresses the audience as though they are the people of the town.*

SHERIFF OF NOTTINGHAM TAX TIME PEOPLE! PAY UP! PAY UP! YOU KNOW WHAT TIME IT IS, TAX TIME YOU CHIRPY LITTLE CHERUB-FACED ANGELS!

MESSENGER Yeah come along you Angels! *Angels*?

SHERIFF OF NOTTINGHAM NORMAL SERVICE, IN AID OF SPEEDINESS AND SANITISATION, HAVE YOUR COINS READY, PUR-LEASE, SAVES ME HAVING TO SNATCH THEM OUT OF YOUR SWEATY LITTLE DISEASE-RIDDEN PAWS. THANK YOU.

MESSENGER Yeah.

SHERIFF OF NOTTINGHAM (*to* **MESSENGER**) If you're gonna talk can you bring something to the table that's actually helpful.

MESSENGER What do you mean?

SHERIFF OF NOTTINGHAM Well it's just this 'Yeah' business, what's that all about? It's not working for me.

MESSENGER It's just a hype man thing, for encouragement, that's what they do so... It's legit.

SHERIFF OF NOTTINGHAM Hype man? I am my own 'hype man' thank you. You just keep your mouth closed very firmly extremely shut and take the coins off the poor people. EUGH. They stink.

SHERIFF *talks again into his megaphone.*

DON'T ANY OF YOU PEOPLE WASH? EVER HEARD OF DEODORANT? I CAN HIGHLY RECOMMEND A ROLL-ON, BETTER FOR THE ENVIRONMENT AND AVOIDS CHAFFING.

SHERIFF *to* **MESSENGER**.

Don't suppose any of these lot have an instrument lying around, could you ask? I mean, let's be real, I'm not expecting anything fancy, I'm in the mood for a bit of a sing song.

MESSENGER I'm not sure Sheriff. Do you want me to ask?

SHERIFF OF NOTTINGHAM Please.

MESSENGER *goes off.* **SHERIFF** *pretends he works at a fruit and veg market.*

TAXES, TAXES GET YOUR TAXES! I mean, PAY. I get so into character... TAXES, TAXES *PAY* YOUR TAXES!

The **SHERIFF** *tries a bit of beat boxing.*

Should have really rehearsed that in private before coming out in public today.

The **MERRY MANY;** **ALAN-A-DALE** *and* **WILL SCARLET**, *sneak in behind the* **SHERIFF**, *we see them scampering in through back doors, windows, wonky loose floor boards with money bags. They hand out money to the poor with a Shhhhhhh...! Meanwhile the* **SHERIFF** *interacts with the audience, asking them to pay money. The audience distract the* **SHERIFF**.

COME ON DIG DEEP, I KNOW CHRISTMAS IS PENDING BUT THAT'S NO EXCUSE NOT TO COUGH UP WHEN

I HAVE A PLUMP TURKEY OF MY OWN THAT NEEDS STUFFING! I have my eye on a few treats I'd like to get from Father Christmas this year...and I think I've been a VERY good boy, what do you think?

Audience shout NO etc.

Oh and I bet you're all just SUCH goody goodies toffees wouldn't melt aren't you?

The **SHERIFF** *pokes his tongue out at everybody.*

COME ON! PAY UP! PAY UP! WHAT DO YOU MEAN YOU HAVEN'T 'GOT ANY MONEY' You're about 4 and a half years of age, GROW UP, you are completely competent and responsible to earn money and pay your taxes just like the rest of us. Come on, pay up. What about your chocolate coin? You didn't eat it did you? Unbelievable.

The **MESSENGER** *returns.*

MESSENGER The good news is that I could only get you this sir.

The **MESSENGER** *hands the* **SHERIFF** *a Kazoo.*

SHERIFF OF NOTTINGHAM What the FUDGE is that?

MESSENGER Ah, it's a... Kazoo. See, I'll show you.

SHERIFF OF NOTTINGHAM I KNOW WHAT IT IS! I don't want your lick on it thank you very much.

MESSENGER Beg your pardon Sheriff.

SHERIFF *tries the Kazoo.*

SHERIFF OF NOTTINGHAM I wanted to do a big scary death march and scare these Squirmy Wormy Brightly Coloured Jelly Beans! I want a big drum! An electric guitar! An ORGAN! I WANT TO PERPETRATE TERROR AND IGNITE EARTH SHATTERING FEAR THROUGH THEIR BONES! How am I meant to musically translate those type of emotions with *this*?

MESSENGER I'll return it Sheriff.

SHERIFF OF NOTTINGHAM No, no, I'm sure... I...can give it a go. A good workman never blames his tools, an excellent musician never blames his instruments.

SHERIFF *into the megaphone.*

Beggars can't be choosers can they guys?

Music begins.

[MUSIC NO. 6: "TAX SONG (REAL NICE GUY)"]

GATHER ROUND PEOPLE COS THE SHERIFF'S IN TOWN,
EMPTY OUT YOUR POCKETS, TURN THEM ALL INSIDE OUT,
I'M A REAL NICE GUY, I'M HONEST AND UPFRONT
I'M A REAL NICE GUY AND YOUR MONEY'S WHAT I WANT.

FORGET ABOUT YOUR HEATING COS I NEED A NEW CAR
YOU CAN ALL BE FREEZING AS I SMOKE MY CIGARS
I'M A REAL NICE GUY, I'M HONEST AND UPFRONT
I'M A REAL NICE GUY AND YOUR MONEY'S WHAT I WANT.

HOLES IN YOUR CLOTHES I GOT A BRAND NEW FUR COAT
GO BAREFOOT TO WORK I GOT MYSELF A SPEEDBOAT
BUT I'M A REAL NICE GUY, I'M HONEST AND UPFRONT,
I'M A REAL NICE GUY AND YOUR MONEY'S WHAT I WANT.

YOU CAN'T AFFORD TO DRINK AND YOU'VE NOTHING TO EAT
WHILST I PAY A STRANGER TO PEDICURE MY FEET
I'M A REAL NICE GUY I'M HONEST AND UPFRONT
I'M A REAL NICE GUY AND YOUR MONEYS WHAT I WANT.

SO HAND OVER YOUR MONEY COS THE SHERIFF'S IN TOWN
WHILE YOU'RE GETTING FIRED I'M NEXT IN LINE FOR THE
    CROWN
I'M A REAL NICE GUY, I'M HONEST AND UPFRONT
I'M A REAL NICE GUY AND YOUR MONEYS WHAT I WANT.

COME A LITTLE CLOSER, COME ON IF YOU DARE
I'LL TAKE AWAY YOUR FREEDOM AND PUT A PRICE ON THE
   AIR
I'M A REAL NICE GUY, I'M HONEST AND UPFRONT
I'M A REAL NICE GUY AND YOUR MONEYS WHAT I WANT.

Well me, oh, my, oh, my, oh, me, oh, my. Looky wooky what
we have here. If it isn't Will Scarlet. A Wanted Man with a
price upon his head. YUM. YUM. You know, Will Scarlet,
we've been offering money to these *Cutie Pies* to catch you
in a trap, that's where the tax payers-money goes. See if
it wasn't for *Pesky Cinnamon-Doused Strudels* like you
breaking the law all the time the taxes wouldn't have to be
so high. So... I suppose...in a way...you're sort of to blame
for the poverty in this cruddy little town.

WILL SCARLET NO! I HELP THE PEOPLE! YOU'RE TO
BLAME!

SHERIFF OF NOTTINGHAM Nice to see where your money
goes isn't it champs? Well spent. And seeing as though *I*
captured you I guess I'll keep the tax money for MYSELF!
My incentive for keeping *Bouquets of Flowers* like you off
the streets. It's nice to be rewarded for ones hardwork.
GUARD! CHAIN THIS ROTTEN OUTLAW CRIMINAL
WILL SCARLET UP AT ONCE!

WILL SCARLET *struggles, fighting for his life.* **GUARDS**
capture and cuff **WILL SCARLET**. *They wrap his mouth
with a gag. The* **SHERIFF** *grabs* **WILL SCARLET** *by the
face and holds him out to the audience.*

Tut. Tut. Tut. RISKING YOUR LIFE FOR A BUNCH OF
WORTHLESS HUMPTY DUMPTIES , eh? I'VE SEEN
DIRTY NAPPIES MORE WORTH SAVING THAN THESE
PENNILESS POPCORN-KERNELLED PARASITES! Will,
Will. Look, you can do better than these *Lollipop*heads. I'm
disappointed in you. But alas, you've carved your fate and
now, William, you're off for a charming stay in a stone-cold
concrete tower with NO water and NO food and only a
SMALL box window to look out at the world from. Where

the bed is straw and little tiddly mice nibble at your cheesy toes. IT'S CALLED PRISON BOIIIIIIII! But don't worry, you won't be there for long, it's just a short stay, because you're next vacation will be a one way ticket to eternal, everlasting, neverending planet hell called DEATH. So there. MU-HA-MU-HA-MU...

The **SHERIFF** *splutters and coughs. Talking to the townsfok...*

Oh shut up you lot. You're no better. Risking your own livelihoods to be bum-chummy best pals with a bunch of Merry Many loser crooks. You do all realise that that's STOLEN money that you're taking from them. And well, by my books that makes you all loser crooks too. I'd hang you all if I had enough rope. Or if I could be BOTHERED to dig your ugly graves. So instead I'll leave you all with a punishment. That will end up killing you nice and slowly anyway. The next time I come to collect tax from you Bunch of *Perfectly-Toasted Melty Cheese Toasties* –

MESSENGER Sorry Sheriff – Can I just –

SHERIFF OF NOTTINGHAM WHAT NOW you *Warmth of a Much-Needed Grandma Hug?*

MESSENGER I – I...it's just... I have to tell you, you know these "offensive terms" you've been using –

SHERIFF OF NOTTINGHAM Please don't drop "" *(gestures inverted commas with hands)* in my presence.

MESSENGER Sorry, Sheriff, it's just...woah there, are you ok? Your eyes are making me nervous...

SHERIFF OF NOTTINGHAM What? It's just my face, I do have an intimidating resting face.

MESSENGER No, not intimidating more...derranged. Anyway. It's just you know these offensive terms –

SHERIFF OF NOTTINGHAM What about them?

MESSENGER I mean, it's great to see you've been putting them into practise but it's just *some* of them aren't really offensive curses at all, in fact *some* of them...come across as compliments?

SHERIFF OF NOTTINGHAM Compliments? Please tell me how a *Cheese Toastie* is a compliment?

MESSENGER Well people like a good cheese toastie don't they?

SHERIFF OF NOTTINGHAM Not a dairy free lactose intolerant people... I mean person...doesn't.

MESSENGER Or a *Grandma Hug*...

SHERIFF OF NOTTINGHAM Errr... What are you talking about everybody? EVERYBODY HATES A GRANDMA HUG! EVERYBODY. And you listen here, the day I take social skill advice from you, mate, is the day I... I...just look, it won't be happening ok? Now let me get back to PUNISHING –

The MESSENGER *shakes his head.*

Listen up *Babycakes* – the next time I come to collect The Tax it will NOT be the usual tax fare, no, no IT IS RECKONING DAY GIRLFRIENDS and BOYFRIENDS ... And that means... DOUBLE TAX!

Gasp!

MESSENGER Sheriff, double Tax?

SHERIFF OF NOTTINGHAM That's right. DOUBLE!

MESSENGER Are you sure about that?

SHERIFF OF NOTTINGHAM DOUBLE. DOUBLE. In a BUBBLE. Toil and TROUBLE. SCRUBBLE. However it goes. COURSE I'M SURE. That's right. DOUBLE!

MESSENGER But Sheriff that's a LOT of taxes, I don't think the people of Nottingham will be able to keep up with those demands, there will be famine, a –

SHERIFF OF NOTTINGHAM   Well they'll just have to find a way won't they?

To audience.

WON'T YOU? SMUG LITTLE CUTE SAUSAGE-LESS VEGETARIAN PIGLETS! And let's see how swift your trusty loyal superhero Robin Hood comes a-robbin' back to you lot to save the day? And I'LL be waiting! And I shall catch that *Sparkling Symmetrical Snowflake* in action once and for all. Or maybe, *maybe*, she'll just leave you to all fend for yourselves? To rot and die...just like nature intended? We shall see...that's it folks, join us next week on THE HA HA HA YOU'RE SO POOR SHOW!

ALAN-A-DALE *runs off into the woods. The* **SHERIFF** *spots him. The* **MESSENGER** *brings out binoculars.*

Who goes there?

MESSENGER   Think it's another one of those Merry Many Sheriff, looks like Alan-a-Dale to me, he's on the Wanted List also, want me to go after him?

SHERIFF OF NOTTINGHAM   Ha! NO! Let that *Glorious Antique Jewellery-Box* go back to his little bezzie mate sleepover in the woods and report back to Robin Hood what he has witnessed here today, that one of their precious Merry Many is not so MERRY anymore. Right. I am IN-VIG-OR-ATED. Let's bounce. I am outttta here.

End of Act One

ACT TWO

1. Maid Marion

Characters: **FRIAR TUCK, ROBIN HOOD, MAID MARION.**

ROBIN *and the* **FRIAR** *walking up to the castle gates of* **MAID MARION***'s castle.*

FRIAR TUCK Why the maid then?

ROBIN HOOD Because, like you, Friar, she isn't Wanted.

FRIAR TUCK Yes and I'm sure, that *also* like me, the lady would proabaly like to keep it that way.

ROBIN HOOD Oh please. She's a 'lady of the house' and you're a Friar. You're like gold dust you two. You are never gonna be the Cover Girl... I mean 'face of' ...a Wanted Poster are you?

FRIAR TUCK Why is she going to want to help these people, Robin? It's risking her life.

ROBIN HOOD Because she will surely want to help the poor. She knows what hardships Nottingham is under. And because we're old friends. You help them out. That's what old friends do.

FRIAR TUCK And what if she doesn't remember you?

ROBIN HOOD Oh sorry, I didn't realise I was being interviewed by the Local Gazette. She just will, alright? She LOVES me. We go way, way, way back. We were like BFF's. Always together. Finishing off each other's sentences, sharing from the same packet of crisps, plaiting each others hair, that kind of thing.

FRIAR TUCK Well let's see. I suppose you are pretty difficult to forget.

The pair walk past another of **ROBIN**'s *Wanted posters...*

ROBIN HOOD Exactly. You better get used to that.

A person walks past, looks at the poster and then at **ROBIN**. **ROBIN** *puffs her chest out, the person walks straight past.*

DON'T ASK FOR AN AUTOGRAPH THEN!

ROBIN *is about to knock...*

Oh, Friar. Probably best if you stay outside though, I haven't seen Marion for a long time and don't exactly know how she'll take to strangers, you know?

FRIAR TUCK Fine. I'll wait here.

ROBIN HOOD Least you've got your Ribena to keep you company, eh? Drink up old boy. For courage.

FRIAR TUCK You've drunk it all Robin.

ROBIN HOOD Ah, shame that. I'll be as quick as I can and then, hopefully, the three of us can blissfully cross-armed-skip back to Sherwood Forest.

ROBIN *rings the grand bell to the castle.* **MARION** *looks down from her tower.* **MARION** *has a ridiculous set of plaits upon her head.*

Marion? Marion? Is that you? LONG TIME GIRL! WHAT YA SAYIN'? It's me. Robin.

MAID MARION Who?

ROBIN *looks embarrassed in front of the* **FRIAR**.

ROBIN HOOD ROBIN. FROM BACK IN THE DAY? ROBBY. LIL' BOB. ROBIN HOOD?

MAID MARION Robin Hood? Absolutely not. I hate you. Don't come back here. Goodbye.

Exit **MAID MARION**. *The* **FRIAR** *tries not to laugh.*

FRIAR TUCK Oh but she loves you. You go way way *way* back.

ROBIN HOOD Shut it Friar.

ROBIN *knocks again.*

Marion, please – I know we had our differences but that was in the past, I'm a different person now, honestly.

MARION *does not come to the window.*

Look, I'm sorry if I ever did anything that ever hurt or upset you, I really truly am. I was a spoilt rotten kid but in hindsight, you weren't always a total babe yourself now were you?

A bucket of water slings down and lands all over **ROBIN**'s *head. The* **FRIAR** *snorts with laughter.*

Ok. I deserved that.

FRIAR TUCK What did you do *girl*?

ROBIN HOOD Stay out of this, Friar.

FRIAR TUCK And to think I carried you across a body of water...

ROBIN HOOD Marion. I made some mistakes in the past. I know I did. But please, I'm trying to make up for all of that. I've had time away, a lot of time actually. I've had a lot of growing up to do. And this time, I think, no, *I know*, that I am actually making a difference, doing something good with myself that isn't selfish. Look, I just came to see how you were doing after all of these years but also to see if you wanted to maybe help make a difference too...

MARION *appears over her tower.*

MAID MARION If you think that after all these years you can just roll up here with all your – Hold on, no way, FRIAR? FRIAR TUCK IS THAT YOU?

FRIAR TUCK Pardon me, have we met?

MAID MARION You don't know me but I know you!

FRIAR TUCK You do?

MAID MARION Yeah, I love your Good Work, honestly. I'm a massive fan. I've heard you speak many a time in town. And your passages, you write so well.

ROBIN *looks so shocked.*

FRIAR TUCK Oh well, that's very kind of you to say so.

MAID MARION Gosh, so what you doing hanging out with this trollop then?

ROBIN HOOD Trollop?

FRIAR TUCK Must be honest, I've sort of been asking myself the same question.

ROBIN HOOD WHAT?

MAID MARION You must come in for tea –

FRIAR TUCK I shall.

MAID MARION And... YES, *you can come too Robin*, but only because you keep such good company.

ROBIN HOOD Oh cheers.

MAID MARION But if you annoy me *once* I'll get my guards to kick you and that bow and arrow of yours all the way back to wherever you've been lurking the last few years.

ROBIN HOOD Well it's great to see you too. Glad to see you haven't changed a bit.

The door to the castle opens up.

FRIAR TUCK After you, Lil' Bob.

2. Meeting Maid Marion

Characters: **ROBIN HOOD, MAID MARION, FRIAR TUCK.**

ROBIN *and the* **FRIAR** *follow* **MARION** *into her castle where she has been stitching. A big pile of ragdolls sit in a big basket. Fabric, fluff, string.*

MARION *pours out tea as* **ROBIN** *looks about, nosily.*

ROBIN HOOD What are these dolls all about then?

MAID MARION I made them.

ROBIN HOOD What are they, Voodoo dolls?

MAID MARION Obviously not Robin or you'd be dead by now.

ROBIN HOOD Charming. What are they for then?

MAID MARION I make them for the children. In Nottingham. To hand out. Nobody has anything to spare anymore with the taxes. It's not the children's fault. They shouldn't have to suffer.

ROBIN HOOD That's very nice of you, which is why we've come actually –

MAID MARION Oh save your sarcasm Robin please, I don't need your pity or praise.

ROBIN HOOD I'm being serious, I wanted to –

MAID MARION So tell me Friar, of your recent work...

ROBIN HOOD It's mostly a lot of pie guzzling and Ribena glugging isn't it Tuck?

FRIAR TUCK No, it is not it's –

MAID MARION Why can't you just let a person speak for themselves?

ROBIN HOOD I was only joking –

MAID MARION Thought jokes are meant to be funny.

ROBIN HOOD Oh here we go.

MAID MARION I knew you'd be rude, you always were, you just can't help yourself. You're a horrible mean bully of a girl that thinks she's so much better than everyone else.

FRIAR TUCK Horrible horrible girl.

ROBIN HOOD FRIAR?

MAID MARION She is. She always talks for everybody, interrupts, very rude. You know Friar, we went to school together and Robin would sit behind me in class and every time I put my hand up to speak she would butt in and try and finish off my sentences, to look like *she* knew the answers to stuff.

ROBIN HOOD Hang on! I am here you know!

The **FRIAR** *joins in, winding* **ROBIN** *up.*

FRIAR TUCK That's not very nice Robin. Shame on you.

MAID MARION And, guess what else she did? She'd steal from my packet of crisps.

ROBIN HOOD What? That's just petty!

FRIAR TUCK NEVER!

MAID MARION SHE WOULD!

FRIAR TUCK ROBIN!

ROBIN HOOD I never!

MAID MARION You stole my crisps and you know it.

ROBIN HOOD Oh once, maybe, I stole *a* crisp. As a joke. To wind you up.

MAID MARION ONCE? Every day more like.

ROBIN HOOD No way, you always had prawn cocktail, I hate prawn cocktail.

MAID MARION The only reason I had prawn cocktail was because IT WAS THE ONLY FLAVOUR YOU WOULDN'T STEAL!

ROBIN HOOD Oh this is getting silly now.

FRIAR TUCK I quite like it.

MAID MARION But the worst, very worst, thing you did, out of *all* the things, ohhhh, now this, this Friar, will make you so mad you might, ooooo this is bad...

> **MAID MARION** *gets pumped up...*

FRIAR TUCK Oh go on Marion, do tell... I'm listening...

> *The* **FRIAR** *leans back comfortably in his chair, legs folded.*

ROBIN HOOD Oh what's this now? What did I do this time? *Breathe* near you?

MAID MARION I'll tell you what you did, one lunch time –

ROBIN HOOD Oh not this one.

MAID MARION Yes *this* one. One lunch time –

ROBIN HOOD You remember it wrong, she remembers it wrong, Friar.

MAID MARION How could I remember it wrong, it scarred me for life.

ROBIN HOOD Here we go...

MAID MARION One lunch time, after I refused to help you with your maths homework –

ROBIN HOOD You mean after *you* deliberately spilled strawberry milk OVER my maths homework?

MAID MARION You jogged me!

ROBIN HOOD I DID NOT!

MAID MARION Guess what MY GREAT FRIEND Robin Hood did?

ROBIN HOOD It's not true Friar, none of this is...

FRIAR TUCK Let the girl speak.

MAID MARION She marched me up the field with that bow and arrow of hers –

ROBIN HOOD It was a PLASTIC one at the time, a training one, with rubber suckers!

MAID MARION Yes and it was VERY threatening I'll have you know.

FRIAR TUCK Go on...

MAID MARION Then she tied my hands behind my back, dragged me to the high fence and then took it upon herself to undo my plaits and re-plait them to the school railings!

FRIAR TUCK ROBIN!

>   **FRIAR** *is finding it hard not to laugh.*

ROBIN HOOD I DID NOT!

FRIAR TUCK HOW COULD YOU?

ROBIN HOOD She's embroidering the truth now, Friar, with her stitches of lies.

MAID MARION And I spent all lunch time there, screaming my head off.

>   *The* **FRIAR** *is loving this, winding up* **ROBIN** *is bringing him great amusement.*

FRIAR TUCK OH NO!

ROBIN HOOD The screaming bit's true. All you did was make noise. Anyway it wasn't ALL lunch time.

FRIAR TUCK Did you miss lunch? Did you get to eat?

MAID MARION Not a single scrap.

ROBIN HOOD Oh please.

FRIAR TUCK Poor girl.

MAID MARION *gets teary. Loving the attention.*

MAID MARION And it was Friday and everything.

FRIAR TUCK Friday?

ROBIN HOOD What does that *even* mean?

MAID MARION *(squealing)* Fishfingers, chips and beans day.

FRIAR TUCK *gasps.*

ROBIN HOOD This is NOT how it went Friar...listen...

[MUSIC NO. 7: "WE WERE ONCE FRIENDS"]

WE WERE ONCE FRIENDS, THAT BIT'S TRUE,
THERE WAS A FENCE, YOU WERE *BRIEFLY* TIED TO,
BUT THAT DOESN'T MEAN... I DID IT TO YOU,
SOMETIMES FENCES, LIKE FRIENDS, YEAH...THEY CAN UNDO.

FRIAR TUCK No, Robin, not another one of your songs... Marion,
I can't deal with the song thing. I don't suppose you have
anything stronger to slop into this tea?

MAID MARION

YOU EMBARRASSED ME, YOU CALLED ME NAMES,
MADE FUN OF MY FUN AND MY GAMES,
YOU GAVE ME TEARS,
YOU GAVE ME SHAME,
AND SO IT APPEARS, MY DEAR, WE CAN'T BE FRIENDS AGAIN.

ROBIN HOOD

NO, NO, NO, YOU REMEMBER IT WRONG,
I WANTED TO PLAY WITH YOU BUT YOU'D STRING ME ALONG.

MAID MARION

HA, HA, NO WAY, NOW THE TIME HAS ALL GONE,
I ONLY WANTED TO HIDE WITH YOU BUT YOU'D SAY...GET
      LOST.

ROBIN HOOD

YOU KNEW IT ALL, YOU WERE SO SMUG,
JUST COS YOU KNEW, THIS FANCY STUFF,

YOU MADE ME FEEL NOT GOOD ENOUGH,
AND YOU LIKED IT A BIT, ADMIT IT, WHEN I GOT TOLD OFF.

MAID MARION
YOU WERE SO RUDE AND SO ROUGH,
STRUTTING AROUND LIKE YOU WERE TOUGH,
YOU WERE A BULLY, A SHOW OFF,
SO DON'T BLAME ME FOR NOT LIKING YOU...VERY MUCH.

ROBIN HOOD So I see you're still patronising,

I tried to make a mends today but you're not having it.

MAID MARION No, I won't, this is no apology,

I only wanted to be your friend but you didn't want to...be friends with me.

ROBIN HOOD Why can't we just be friends, why can't we just be friends, why can't we just be friends, now or never?

MAID MARION We will *never* be friends. I don't *wanna* be friends. We will *never* be friends. NEVER again.

ROBIN HOOD Why can't be just be friends?

MAID MARION We will *never* be friends.

ROBIN HOOD Why can't we just be friends?

MAID MARION I don't *wanna* be friends.

ROBIN HOOD Why can't we just be friends?

MAID MARION We will *never* be friends.

ROBIN HOOD Now or never?

MAID MARION Never again.

ROBIN HOOD You're uptight, twisted, cling on to the bad bits.

MAID MARION Class yourself a misfit just to get some kindness.

ROBIN HOOD You're righteous, pedantic, small minded and frantic.

MAID MARION Least I don't hug trees and act like I'm some bad chick.

ROBIN HOOD You're lonely. Judgemental.

MAID MARION Least I'm not mental.

ROBIN HOOD You're spiteful and rude –

MAID MARION You act like a dude!

ROBIN HOOD You live in a bubble –

MAID MARION WELL YOU'RE PLAIN HORRIBLE. And that's why I don't LIKE you!

ROBIN HOOD And that's why I DON'T CARE

MAID MARION YOU HAVE A BAD ATTITUDE!

ROBIN HOOD WELL YOU HAVE BAD HAIR!

The pair launch at each other into a scrap.

3. Prison Cell

Characters: **WILL SCARLET, SHERIFF, GUARDS.**

In a horrible, dark, dingy, damp cell. **WILL SCARLET** *is chained to the walls, he is angry. There are the sounds of screams, of echoing emptiness and nothingness, the freezing howling wind and the scampering and rustling, the clank of metal.*

A key in the lock, twists, **WILL SCARLET** *prepares himself. The* **SHERIFF** *enters holding a flaming torch. His* **GUARDS** *behind him.*

SHERIFF OF NOTTINGHAM This morning I woke up and I thought, alas, just another day of fine wine, stinky cheese, greasy pigs' trotters, perhaps a bit of backslapping with the boys, ego boosting and general Banty McBantyson but *oh no, no, no*...how mistaken I was, I clearly had my 'not my best ones' sunglasses on and underestimated the day... because then I captured you.

WILL SCARLET What do you want Sheriff? If you're going to kill me just do it now. I feel dead anyway.

SHERIFF OF NOTTINGHAM Oh you feel dead do you? Nothing on the inside? Howling gut and the sense of imprisonment got you down? Well that's what happens when you *Make a Crime.* You Get A Punish-Ment. Don't you see Will? I don't want to kill you if you, and I quote, 'feel dead anyway'. BORING. Where's the fun in that for me, hmm? I wonder... how could we make you feel a bit...less dead? Guards, what do we reckon?

WILL SCARLET *wrestles with the chains as the* **GUARDS** *approach him.*

WILL SCARLET No, no, not torture, no, no. NO!

SHERIFF OF NOTTINGHAM Oh yes, yes, yes. Stretttttchiinngggg until your ribcage explodes out of your chest? And your arms and legs crack, string out like runner beans?

WILL SCARLET No! No! Sheriff, have mercy!

SHERIFF OF NOTTINGHAM Spiked Walls? No, *Spiked Tomb*? TOMB! Yes! Might die of the bones breaking or suffocation before you bleed to death...holes everywhere, you'll never be able to eat a bowl of tomato soup again without it whooshing out of you like a colander!

WILL SCARLET PLEASE, PLEASE!

SHERIFF OF NOTTINGHAM Or caged, left to hang up for the crows to peck you to smoosh, very dramatic, right crowd – pleaser that, they start with the squashy bits first – eyeballs, tongue, brain. Until they get to the rotten entrails. Then hack at the bone... Use it to sharpen their beaks. Sound fun? More up your street? Might get you feeling a bit more...alive?

WILL SCARLET No, please, please, I won't do anything wrong again, I swear I won't...

SHERIFF OF NOTTINGHAM Or... Glitter Bomb.

WILL SCARLET Glitter Bom –?

SHERIFF OF NOTTINGHAM Oh my word have you never heard of a Glitter Bomb? So good. You will die, not in that way, well you might, out of AMAZEMENT!

(Or if you're of a faint-hearted nature, sensitive to practical jokes or susceptible to heart attacks via the form of MEGA LOLZ.) Basically, what it is, comes in card form or canister, send it to an enemy's house, by post is fine, the receiver opens it and then BAM-AGH! GLITTER, glitter pouring out, total glitter avalanche and let me tell you it goes EVERYWHERE. Eyebrows, nostrils, cereal...

WILL SCARLET That sounds terrible. PLEASE, NONE OF THE ABOVE.

WILL *suddenly freaks out.*

SHERIFF OF NOTTINGHAM William, Willy, Willy... WILL ...
Nobody is going to torture anybody, not now anyway.

The **SHERIFF** *nods to his* **GUARDS** *to unlock* **WILL.** **WILL**
rubs his wrists.

Bud, calm down, this should take the edge off, cool you
down...

The **SHERIFF** *offers* **WILL** *a drink from his flask.* **WILL**
looks suspicious.

Oh, ok, and I'd poison you now would I? Because that's
exactly the kind of cowardly way somebody like me would
kill a man.

The **SHERIFF** *considers the thought.*

Suppose it is really, hadn't really considered poison before.

WILL *has a gulp from the* **SHERIFFS** *flask –.*

IT'S POISON!

WILL *spits it out.*

It's not. It's not poison. Couldn't resist. *So* got you then.
Classic. Drink it, it's fine.

WILL *drinks again, staring the* **SHERIFF** *out.*

Oooo, he drinks from the devil's cup. And it calms the man
down like...yoghurt to a curry.

The **SHERIFF** *sits next to* **WILL.**

Sooo... Oh this is nice, cosy, look at us sitting here like
friends, could be anywhere couldn't we, almost forget the
whole, 'Prison setting.' Just two old mates; *what you been
up to recently mate, ahhh, we're so close, we tell each other
everything, wanna come to my birthday party?* Haha. No.
Imagine. I mean you're welcome to come to my party, it's next
month but...you probably don't want – wouldn't want to –

WILL *seems reluctant.*

Give me that.

The SHERIFF *snatches back his flask.*

Wow. How much did you drink, hoggy hoggerson? Backwashed it as well I bet. Typical. Typical, Will that is guards. Corr dear. Will, what if I was to...let you go? Right now, goodbye, shake hands, BAM, free man?

WILL SCARLET Let me go? Why would you do that?

SHERIFF OF NOTTINGHAM Well obviously there's got to be something in it for me...

WILL SCARLET What?

SHERIFF OF NOTTINGHAM *Ahhh, you become my best friend? Or something...* Lols. Joking. Obvs. Robin Hood.

WILL SCARLET What about her?

SHERIFF OF NOTTINGHAM I want her. She is a *Fluffy-Clouded Goddess of Fierceness* and I DESPISE her! I want her dead.

WILL SCARLET No. Forget it. Lock me back up. I won't do it.

SHERIFF OF NOTTINGHAM Well she got you arrested in the first place didn't she? She wasn't the one out handing out money to the poor, that was you. In Karma's books, you were just out doing a bit of the old 'do-gooding' really, you shouldn't have to suffer for her actions, she's the criminal in all this. Not you.

WILL SCARLET She promised it would be alright...

SHERIFF OF NOTTINGHAM She forced you is what she did. She can't be trusted. Dignity, class divide, superiority has a system, Will. A hierarchy. It runs through the genes, through the DNA. And your pal, Robin, places herself at the very top of the chain. She doesn't value you. She doesn't respect you.

WILL SCARLET I can't capture her and bring her here myself, The Merry Many will kill me.

SHERIFF OF NOTTINGHAM No, no, you wouldn't have to. What if I said I was to remove *that* price off your head? We start from scratch. Call it quits. A truce if you like. Then you really would be a free man. Now *that* Will Scarlet, is a reason to live.

WILL SCARLET What would I have to do?

SHERIFF OF NOTTINGHAM Just, simply, tell me where to find Robin Hood.

WILL SCARLET She was going to see an old friend of hers...

SHERIFF OF NOTTINGHAM Pray do tell...

WILL SCARLET I don't know her, some Maid... Marion or something.

SHERIFF OF NOTTINGHAM Maid Marion? You mean 'the' Maid Marion?

WILL SCARLET That's all I know.

SHERIFF OF NOTTINGHAM I've heard she's pretty fit you know?

WILL SCARLET I really don't – sorry, couldn't comment on that.

SHERIFF OF NOTTINGHAM I didn't know those two had history, that's very interesting indeed... Oh my days... I've just thought of something... Oh my days, oh my days... I could, *literally*, cuddle my own brain right now. This is brilliant, just brilliant.

WILL SCARLET What?

SHERIFF OF NOTTINGHAM I'm not telling you! I only tell things to my messenger or to myself via the mirror.

WILL SCARLET But you're still going to let me go right?

SHERIFF OF NOTTINGHAM Oh I'll let you go alright...and I'll tell you what...you run back to your little campfire and you tell your little *Sweetie Pie* of a pal Robin Hood and her *RADIANT, FEELGOOD BUNCH of Merry Manys* that there is to be a celebration very soon, a ceremony... Because MAMA!

THERE'S GOING TO BE A WEDDING IN NOTTINGHAM. YER BOY IS GETTING MARRIED!

WILL SCARLET You're getting married? Congratulations, I guess To who?

SHERIFF OF NOTTINGHAM To Maid Marion you *IDYLLIC SKYLINE!*

WILL SCARLET Hold on... Did you literally just decide that you were getting married just then, by yourself?

SHERIFF OF NOTTINGHAM Yep. My brain spoke to my mouth and my mouth said EXCELLENT IDEA and I. DO. I. DO. I DO. Wait a sec, why are you not bouncing up and down with ecstatic joy for me?

WILL SCARLET It's just...well...no, no worries, not really my place to say...

SHERIFF OF NOTTINGHAM Go on...if you're going to rain on my parade at least have the nerve to do it properly.

WILL SCARLET Shouldn't you kind of, I dunno –

SHERIFF OF NOTTINGHAM It's just simply to lure Robin into my trap. It's not an actual *love* thing.

WILL SCARLET No, no, I was under no illusion that it was for love, Sheriff, don't you worry about that, it's just...well, shouldn't you ask her if she wants to marry you first before you go round saying you're getting married?

SHERIFF OF NOTTINGHAM Hahahahahahahahahahahahaha hahahahahahahahahahahahahahahahahahahahaha hahahahahah ahahahahahahahahahahahahahahahhaha hhahahahaha. Yes, you're right. I totally should. That's quite presumptuous of me. Guards... GET ME AN UBER, I'M GOING TO MAID MARION'S HOUSE.

The **SHERIFF** *turns to leave...*

And then lock up this *Little Perfectly Baked Raison-Studded Bun* will you?

WILL SCARLET WHAT? NO! YOU TRICKED ME! That's not fair. We made a deal.

The **GUARDS** *begin to lock up* **WILL SCARLET**.

SHERIFF OF NOTTINGHAM Deals don't always work in everyone's favour. Just like Exchange Students, Will Scarlet, life is never a fair exchange.

WILL SCARLET You can't do this, you SAID! YOU PROMISED! YOU SAID WE COULD CALL IT QUITS! YOU'RE A LIAR!

SHERIFF OF NOTTINGHAM There's only one thing worse than a liar Will, and that's somebody who backstabs their friend. Especially, when that friend is Robin Hood. Night, night. Or whatever time it is, I don't own a watch and phones haven't been invented yet.

The door slams behind the **SHERIFF**, *bolting shut, leaving* **WILL** *screaming for his life.*

4. Sherwood Forest

Characters: **ROBIN HOOD, FRIAR TUCK, LITTLE JOHN, ALAN, A MERRY MANY.**

Sombre mood in Sherwood forest. The **MERRY MANY** *are all slumped around looking sad, deflated and empty-handed.* **ALAN** *has told them the news of* **WILL.**

ROBIN *shoots an arrow into the air, it whistles down.* **ROBIN** *arrives through the clearing with a bag of peas/ ice bag over her eye from* **MARION.**

ROBIN HOOD GANG! I'd like you to meet our newest recruit. Merry Many! This is Friar Tuck – Wait, what's wrong with everybody?

LITTLE JOHN She still hates you then?

ROBIN HOOD Oh this? It's just a...little...accident, she hit harder than she intended. Looks worse than it is. So why the sour faces? Little John will you tell me what's the matter with everybody?

LITTLE JOHN Tell her Alan-a-Dale.

ROBIN HOOD Tell me what?

LITTLE JOHN They got Will Scarlet.

ROBIN HOOD The Sheriff? Where has he taken Will?

ALAN-A-DALE He's in a cell for now. But it's certain punishment, by death.

ROBIN HOOD Well what are we all waiting for? We shall go and get him.

LITTLE JOHN It's not as simple as that Robin. Nobody is going to help us, he's doubled the people's tax as punishment for taking money from us, so everybody is too afraid. He's got us cornered.

ROBIN HOOD Rubbish, we can –

LITTLE JOHN No, no, we can't. Not this time. We're one down, Robin. We're lucky Alan got away.

ROBIN HOOD Since when did we cower down and admit defeat? Never o'clock, that's when. WE'RE THE MERRY MANY! Come on we stand up, we fight back –

ALAN-A-DALE Just stop with all your big talk, Robin. Will Scarlet was right about you all along. You aren't one of us. We're just a vanity project for you. Somewhere to cleanse you of your guilt for being so privileged and now our people are suffering because they are taking from *you*. That's our friends and families out there Robin! They can't eat. They can't afford medicine if they get sick! Scarlet...well...he didn't even want to go but you MADE him –

ROBIN HOOD Will Scarlet only thinks for himself, he didn't want to share with –

ALAN-A-DALE You still FORCED him to put his life at risk. Just like how you force us to do whatever you want, you *use* people Robin. Well not anymore.

ROBIN HOOD I don't force anybody to –

ALAN-A-DALE You think you're so much smarter than the rest of us, you boss us all around all the time, thinking you're the leader. Sad thing is, we're the real mugs. Cos we do it. We actually listen to you and all the horse poo that comes out your trap.

ROBIN HOOD Alan, Alan... I...come on, what happened to Sqaud Vibez, eh?

ALAN-A-DALE You swore you'd keep us safe, you *promised* but where were you, eh? When it mattered. Off looking after number one as usual, off making friends it seems –

ROBIN HOOD For us. The Friar is going to help us. The Sheriff isn't suspicious of him, he can –

ALAN-A-DALE You can't help yourself, can you? Just stop it, stop *now*.

ROBIN HOOD I'm trying to help, we have a plan, Friar, don't we? I didn't know there would be – I'm sorry. I'm sorry, I'm sorry we lost our friend.

ALAN-A-DALE *Friend*? Don't use that word near me. I'd run if I was you Friar, she promises you loyalty and protection, no, she promises you the world but she's a fake. She's not your friend. The only person Robin Hood is a friend to, is Robin Hood.

ROBIN HOOD Alan...please...if you can just hear me out... I've got a plan, I swear, I do. I do...

The **MANY** *turn and walk away, grumbling.*

LITTLE JOHN Come on guys, let's build a fire to keep us warm, looks like we won't be going home anytime soon.

ROBIN HOOD John we will, we will. Don't be like that... John? John? John?

LITTLE JOHN *looks at his feet, sad, turning away...*

John. I've let you all down. I'm sorry.

The **FRIAR** *pats* **ROBIN**'s *back.*

FRIAR TUCK You meant well Robin, it wasn't your fault. This time is making everybody desperate. Nobody is themselves.

ROBIN HOOD Alan's right. I swore I would protect them.

ROBIN *gets up and gathers her bow and arrows.*

Oh no, what are you up to now?

I'm going to free Will Scarlet.

FRIAR TUCK How?

ROBIN HOOD I'm going to hand myself in, for Will Scarlet's freedom.

FRIAR TUCK Don't be so preposterous, you can't do that –

ROBIN HOOD Yes I can. I can do anything.

FRIAR TUCK Robin, wait, this is crazy, the Sheriff will kill you. Well won't you let me come with you? You said yourself, the Sheriff won't be suspicious of me, let me at least help you get through his gates?

ROBIN HOOD I appreciate that Friar, but I need to do this alone, I've got you into enough trouble already, I have to prove that I can do this alone.

FRIAR TUCK Robin, you don't have to be a hero *all* the time.

ROBIN HOOD But that's just it Friar, I've never been one to begin with.

FRIAR TUCK Robin! Robin!

ROBIN *exits.*

5. A Proposal

Characters: **SHERIFF, MESSENGER, MAID MARION.**

MARION'*s Castle.*

The **SHERIFF** *and his messenger arrive at* **MARION**'*s castle gates. The* **SHERIFF** *has made an effort to look, what in his opinion, is classed as 'handsome'. He's slicked his hair down and is doing lunges. He has a bouquet in hand and a heart-shaped box of chocolates under his arm.*

SHERIFF OF NOTTINGHAM Right, how do I look?

MESSENGER Kind of like a P.E Teacher going to an award ceremony for the best P.E Teacher, but probably won't win.

SHERIFF OF NOTTINGHAM Oh cheers.

MESSENGER What? That's a compliment, I adored my P.E Teacher.

SHERIFF OF NOTTINGHAM 'Oh I adored my P.E Teacher, blah, blah, blah.' Tell someone who cares. Now, quick, smell my breath?

The **SHERIFF** *blasts his hot air of a breath across the* **MESSENGER**'*s face.*

MESSENGER Ah, the familiar scent of coffee. Hate. Misery. Bitter notes of bitterness. With just a background hint of jealousy and anxiety followed by...is that...Marmite on toast?

SHERIFF OF NOTTINGHAM BOOM! You know that Marmite gives me LIFE boi!

MESSENGER Sure do.

SHERIFF OF NOTTINGHAM Ok, Ok. I'm pumped. I'm ready, I'm ready. Let's do this, let's do this –

SHERIFF *is about to ring the bell and then stops himself.*

Don't you DARE try and stop me.

MESSENGER I won't Sheriff, don't you worry.

SHERIFF OF NOTTINGHAM Don't you dare.

MESSENGER Wouldn't dream of it, Sheriff.

The SHERIFF *goes to ring the bell again. Pauses...*

SHERIFF OF NOTTINGHAM Cos, like, this is a good idea, it's a good idea, isn't it?

MESSENGER It's an *idea*, it's not necessarily a good one but I'd say it certainly isn't a bad one.

SHERIFF OF NOTTINGHAM It's not a good idea is it? Shall we leave it? Leave it yeah. Probs best to leave it, go back to the drawing board and reconvene?

MESSENGER Hmmm... No... I think it will definitely get people talking, get Robin Hood to come to like 'SAVE the day' or whatever.

SHERIFF OF NOTTINGHAM Exactly, exactly, which is what we want. Ok, great. Well without further delay...we shall... I'll just... Ha! I just had this crazy thought, imagine how bad it would be if I was about to ask Robin to marry me instead? Imagine how BAD that would be.

MESSENGER Oh, stop, that's a horrible idea.

SHERIFF OF NOTTINGHAM I don't know why I thought of that just then. What a HORROR story is that? EUGH.

MESSENGER Gross.

SHERIFF OF NOTTINGHAM Imagine that, me marrying Robin Hood. Imagine. Corrr could you imagine? Now, that would be...that would be...what do you reckon *that* would be like? Cos like she's probably a nightmare in real life isn't she? Right pain in the backside...

MESSENGER Oh definitely.

SHERIFF OF NOTTINGHAM Ok. Don't know why I even thought of that. Funny.

The **MESSENGER** *rings the bell. Clang!*

Wait, what are you –?

The **SHERIFF** *licks down his hair and eyebrows, pasting them with spit. The* **MESSENGER** *fusses over the* **SHERIFF**.

Quick, quick, quick, get off, get off, don't, don't, she's coming. Do I look alright? Do I look...

MARION *peers down.*

MAID MARION Hello?

SHERIFF OF NOTTINGHAM Why if it isn't THE Maid Marion?

MESSENGER SICK PLAITS!

MAID MARION Sheriff? (aside to **MESSENGER**): Thanks.

MESSENGER You're welcome.

MAID MARION This is an unexpected visit. Is everything ok? Am I in debt to you? I've paid my taxes.

SHERIFF OF NOTTINGHAM Oh taxes, smaxes, no, no, no, I'm here for much for perkier reasons. I assure you, this time around, and probably *only* this time though, so don't get used to it, my *Plaited Hair Platypus,* it is me, who is indebted to you.

MAID MARION How so? Tax rebate?

SHERIFF OF NOTTINGHAM If you let me come inside...perhaps I can explain?

MAID MARION Hmmm...how did you get my address?

SHERIFF OF NOTTINGHAM Oh just...a friend of a fiend, pointed me in the right direction of your beauty, with whom I'm eternally grateful, by the name of... Will Scarlet.

MAID MARION Will Scarlet? Never heard of him.

SHERIFF OF NOTTINGHAM Ah, he's just an old "friend" of Robin Hood. He's not, he's actually a back-stabbing traitor to be perfectly frank.

MESSENGER *(to* **SHERIFF***)* How comes you get to do the """ *(gestures inverted commas with hands)* and I don't?

SHERIFF OF NOTTINGHAM *(to* **MESSENGER***)* I look cool when I do them, that's why.

MAID MARION I'm sorry, I can't allow strangers inside my castle walls.

SHERIFF OF NOTTINGHAM Strangers? I'm hardly a stranger am I love? I'm only the Sheriff of bloomin' Nottingham.

MAID MARION I get that but I cannot. And besides, impossible, your facts are wrong. This Robin Hood that you speak of, she's no friend of mine.

SHERIFF OF NOTTINGHAM *(to* **MESSENGER***)* I thought they were friends?

MESSENGER *(to* **SHERIFF***)* That's what we were told?

SHERIFF OF NOTTINGHAM *(to* **MESSENGER***)* STUPID SEQUIN-STUDDED EARRINGS! SO ANNOYING, THE WHOLE THING IS WRECKED! What do I do now?

The **SHERIFF** *gets mad but contains himself. The* **MESSENGER** *helps the* **SHERIFF** *keep his cool.*

MESSENGER *(to* **SHERIFF** *through gritted teeth)* Sheriff, stick to the plan.

MESSENGER *beckons on the violins to set the romantic tone.*

SHERIFF OF NOTTINGHAM *(to* **MESSENGER***)* Oh I don't know about this.

MESSENGER *(to* **SHERIFF***)* It's fine, trust me, just keep going.

The violins begin...they only stress the **SHERIFF** *further.*

SHERIFF OF NOTTINGHAM *(to* **MESSENGER***)* Violins? Oh... Not out here, like this. Thought I was going to be inside, didn't

I? Just not how I pictured it, look like an idiot that's all, big deal for me, this.

MESSENGER You're doing great Sheriff.

MAID MARION What's all this about? Are you sure everything is ok?

SHERIFF OF NOTTINGHAM *(to* **MARION***)* Quite sure thank you... nothing to see here... I always roll around with a string band...quartet thingy. For the purpose of theatre and added status.

MESSENGER *(to* **SHERIFF***)* You can do it, just ask her.

SHERIFF OF NOTTINGHAM *(to* **MESSENGER***)* You're right, just ask her – I can't just –

MESSENGER *(to* **SHERIFF***)* Just get down on one knee –

The **MESSENGER** *and* **SHERIFF** *fuss and flap.*

SHERIFF OF NOTTINGHAM *(to* **MESSENGER***)* I can't, my shorts are too short, there's no give, haven't worn them in yet, they're new aren't they? All tight and starched around the old...ouch.

MESSENGER *(to* **SHERIFF***)* Just get down. Just –

SHERIFF OF NOTTINGHAM *(to* **MESSENGER***)* I'm trying, I'm trying, I'm –

MAID MARION What's going on down there?

SHERIFF OF NOTTINGHAM Dear *The* Maid Marion, will you do me the honour of – wait...what do I say?

MESSENGER *(to* **SHERIFF***)* You just say, will you marry me?

SHERIFF OF NOTTINGHAM *(to* **MESSENGER***)* Ha! Oh Sweet Messenger. You didn't think I was marrying *you.* Did you? Ha.

MESSENGER Just. Ask. Her.

MAID MARION Ask me what?

SHERIFF OF NOTTINGHAM Ok, alright, alright, MAID MARION, WILL YOU MARRY ME?

MAID MARION *is shocked, sickened.*

MAID MARION I'm sorry?

SHERIFF OF NOTTINGHAM Marry me? You know. Me and you, tie the knot, why not?

MAID MARION I... I...don't think, Sheriff, that is such a compliment and I am very flattered but we barely know each other, I think it's –

SHERIFF OF NOTTINGHAM You know what? You're completely right, my bad, silly me, sorry to have bothered you, you've got your...plaits and everything...have a lovely day.

MAID MARION *is baffled, the* **MESSENGER** *drags the* **SHERIFF** *back.*

MESSENGER *(to* **SHERIFF***)* Think of Robin, you want her to come to the castle don't you, to rescue Marion?

SHERIFF OF NOTTINGHAM *(to* **MESSENGER***)* I do, but... Ooooooooo. I'm so nervous. I need a poo.

MESSENGER *(to* **SHERIFF***)* Ask.

SHERIFF OF NOTTINGHAM *(to* **MESSENGER***)* But I'm scared.

MESSENGER *(to* **SHERIFF***)* Scared of what?

SHERIFF OF NOTTINGHAM *(to* **MESSENGER***)* Rejection.

MESSENGER *(to* **SHERIFF***)* Look, you're *not* gonna get rejected, AS IF, you're a – really – great...you're a...you've got tons of...qualities...

SHERIFF OF NOTTINGHAM *(to* **MESSENGER***)* Do I? Like what?

MESSENGER *(to* **SHERIFF***)* Like...you're really...errrrmmmm... ok, WHEN she rejects you, here's what you do.

SHERIFF OF NOTTINGHAM *(to* **MESSENGER***)* Go on...

MESSENGER *(to* **SHERIFF***)* You don't ask her again. You TELL her.

The **SHERIFF** *sniggers, getting his mojo back.*

SHERIFF OF NOTTINGHAM *(to* **MESSENGER***)* Tell? *Tell* you say, tell is good.

MESSENGER *(to* **SHERIFF***)* You see? There we go.

SHERIFF OF NOTTINGHAM *(to* **MESSENGER***)* I can do telling. I'm good at telling.

MESSENGER Oh the very best. I'll ask the violinists to leave...

SHERIFF OF NOTTINGHAM No, no...don't –

To violinists...

Don't suppose you could play something a little less, romantically eurphorically charged and instead whip up something more threatening, menacing verging on horror film? Sort of slasher psycho shark attack vibes are fine.

The violinists, although baffled, do as instructed. The **SHERIFF** *loves it.*

Maid Marion. I'm sorry, I think it made it almost seem for a second like you had a chance to turn down the offer of being my wife. Perhaps I wasn't clear? This isn't really one of those little quiz things you do in your girly magazines where one has options, you see, no, you don't get a choice in the matter. You are going to be my wife whether you like it or not. I am ordering you to marry me.

[MUSIC NO. 8: "PROPOSAL SONG"]

THIS ISN'T LOVE,
IT NEVER WAS,
I DON'T EVEN FANCY YOU,
VERY MUCH
BUT YOU'RE GOING TO BE MY WIFE
AND YOU DON'T HAVE A CHOICE.
FRIED EGGS FOR BREAKFAST,

SCRAMBLED FOR LUNCH,
AND IF I'M WORKING AWAY,
YOU'LL MAKE ME PACKED LUNCH,
COS YOU'RE GOING TO BE MY BRIDE
AND YOU DON'T HAVE A CHOICE,
SPANKING CLEAN BATHROOM,
YOU'LL IRON MY SHIRT
AND HANG OUT THE WASHING,
IN YOUR SHORTEST SKIRT
AND YOU'RE GOING TO BE MY WIFE AND YOU DON'T HAVE A
    CHOICE,
I'LL HOST A PARTY AND
YOU'LL DO THE WORK,
AND HAND OUT MINI SAUSAGES
AND LAUGH AT MY JOKES,
COS YOU'RE GONNA BE MY BRIDE,
AND YOU DON'T HAVE A CHOICE, PICTURE THE SCENE HONEY,
    YOU AND ME LYING ON A GRASSY FIELD,
SIPPING ON LUSCIOUS WINE FROM OUR GOLD GOBLETS,
    WATCHING THE WORLD GO BY, ME, EXTREMELY
GOOD LOOKING AND VERY STINKING RICH AND THEN WE
    WILL WONDER BACK TO OUR MANSION CASTLE
WITH OUR CHILDREN- NO SCRAP THAT, I HATE KIDS.

MAID MARION You can't do that.

SHERIFF OF NOTTINGHAM Oh I can. I'm the Sheriff of
Nottingham. I can do what I like, like... I can literally just
walk in any McDonalds and get served.

MAID MARION Anyone can do that.

SHERIFF OF NOTTINGHAM Well, I *really, seriously* can.

MAID MARION Well what if I was to say no?

SHERIFF OF NOTTINGHAM No. You don't say no. No! Hear
that loyal messenger? Mrs Sheriff of Nottingham is testing
my patience, she's trying to say no? Ha...well we shall see
about that.

The **SHERIFF** *suddenly switches and becomes nasty, he climbs up the castle walls towards* **MARION**. *Grunting. Like a deranged wolf.*

MAID MARION Ok, Ok, I accept, I accept. No need to come up. I accept.

SHERIFF OF NOTTINGHAM You do?

MAID MARION I do. I will...be your wife.

SHERIFF OF NOTTINGHAM BOSH! GET IN! Well that is just splendid news! Come down, my fair lady, my delight, my can of Sprite and let us run back to my cold horrible scraggy little bedroom.

MAID MARION Ok, well, won't you let me just get my things?

SHERIFF OF NOTTINGHAM What things could you possibly need? I have everything any woman could possibly want.

MAID MARION Got knickers for every day of the week do you? And a lifetime supply of glittery nail varnish. *(And a cleaver – spoken aside)*

SHERIFF OF NOTTINGHAM Take as long as you need, my rose petal.

The **SHERIFF** *climbs back from the wall and* **MARION** *disappears.*

Oh *The* Maid Marion. You've made me an *almost* happy man. I might be able to even DO a smile. I am rich you know, I've just doubled the taxes, we will have a mighty fine life you and I.

The **MESSENGER** *and* **SHERIFF** *high five each other.*

MESSENGER Nice work, Sheriff.

SHERIFF OF NOTTINGHAM Piece of cake really, don't know why you made such a big fuss about it. Yeah, chuffed with that result bud. About time I settled down, made a man of myself.

MESSENGER Indeed.

SHERIFF OF NOTTINGHAM I suppose you'll be wanting to be the Best Man won't you? Nag. Nag. Nag.

MESSENGER Errr...not especially.

SHERIFF OF NOTTINGHAM Yeah. Yeah, course you will, I know you, begging for it, you'll be right up in there planning the old stag do knees-up with the boys –

MESSENGER Hmm...wouldn't exactly be –

SHERIFF OF NOTTINGHAM If you don't want to do it. Just say. I mean there are numerous people I could ask, got heaps and heaps of blokey boyfriends I could ask, but no, I think... so things don't get nasty, make the others jealous and save you getting all upset etc, it will have to be you.

We see **MARION**, *hitch up her skirt, hoist herself over the wall and sneakily clamber out of the castle, running away with her basket of dolls.*

MESSENGER If I'm not doing anything, then yes, I suppose I *could* be the Best Man.

SHERIFF OF NOTTINGHAM Oh yeah, yeah, course, course, it's a big ask, I get that, check your diary.

MESSENGER Will do.

SHERIFF OF NOTTINGHAM Just don't leave it *too* long. You know, I saw an unmistakable twinkle in her eye. I really think she likes me.

MARION *has vanished. They awkwardly wait.*

She's not coming back is she?

MESSENGER Gotta be honest, I don't think she is, Sheriff, no.

The pair strop off.

6. A Maid, A Friar And Some Merry Dolls

Characters: **MAID MARION, FRIAR TUCK, LITTLE JOHN, ALAN, MERRY MANY.**

Back in Sherwood Forest.

MARION *arrives to find the* **FRIAR.**

MAID MARION Friar, Friar, have you seen Robin?

FRIAR TUCK She's gone.

MAID MARION I want to help, I want to help. I have an idea of how we can –

The **MERRY MANY** *approach.*

FRIAR TUCK Oh dear no.

ALAN-A-DALE Who are you?

FRIAR TUCK This is Maid Mari –

MAID MARION My name is Maid Marion.

ALAN-A-DALE You say it like it's meant to mean something. Didn't ask your name, asked WHO you were.

LITTLE JOHN She's a friend of Robin's.

FRIAR TUCK Well actually, I really wouldn't say they were friends per se, more...

MAID MARION I can't stand the cow.

The **MERRY MANY** *grumble.*

But I like what she's doing, she's helping people, she's kind. She's good.

ALAN-A-DALE Sounds to us like you LIKE her.

MAID MARION Quite the opposite. But if there's one person I hate more than her, it's that Sheriff. And if Robin's taking that Rancid Salad down, then I want to be a part of that.

LITTLE JOHN Where's Robin anyway?

ALAN-A-DALE Who gives a rat's bum?

FRIAR TUCK She's gone to save Will Scarlet.

MAID MARION Will Scarlet? Why do I know that name?

FRIAR TUCK She's going to turn herself in to free him.

LITTLE JOHN Oh Robin.

ALAN-A-DALE Don't feel sorry for her, John. Robin's the reason
Will's locked up in the first place.

LITTLE JOHN Alan, we were all a part of the same scheme,
nobody got their hands more dirty than Robin. And as for
Will, he never wanted to share in the first place. He got
caught because he got unlucky, not because of Robin. You
made it out didn't you?

MAID MARION WILL SCARLET! I know that name, he's the
one that told the Sheriff where I was! He's a traitor! Robin
shouldn't give up her freedom for his.

The **MANY** *react.*

You can't trust him, quick we've got to get a move on. I've
got a plan.

ALAN-A-DALE Oh, no, now *this one's* got a plan. Course she
has. NO MORE PLANS PLEASE!

LITTLE JOHN Go on Maid Marion. By the way, do you want us
to always say Maid at the start or just...

MAID MARION Marion's fine, I much prefer Marion. And what
about you, I mean, do you even like *Little* at the start of
your name because well, obviously you're like MASSIVE,
so, I mean, what's the *deal* with that? Is it irony or...

LITTLE JOHN What do you mean? I know I'm not *little* but I'm
not exactly big am I? I'm just big-boned but I wouldn't say
I was *big* big.

MAID MARION Oh right. No, no, of course.

LITTLE JOHN These are just hormones, padding me out, it's a condition.

MAID MARION Uh huh. Yup.

FRIAR TUCK So what's the plan Marion?

MAID MARION The taxes are doubling right? We need a safe way we can smuggle money to the poor...Well we can smuggle them in, safely.

FRIAR TUCK Smuggle how?

MAID MARION The dolls. The ones I hand out to the children. We can sew the coins into the stuffing, stitch them back up, nobody will know any different.

FRIAR TUCK EXCELLENT! Marion that is perfect!

ALAN-A-DALE But someone's still gotta hand them out? How we going to do that without getting caught?

FRIAR TUCK Ahh, well both Marion and I are known for our do-gooding, it would look quite legitimate, we are always knocking on the doors of the poor offering our aid, neither of us are wanted.

MAID MARION Ahh, well, yes, about that...long story but how do I put this...how about...say for example...

MAID MARION *mumbles really quickly, almost inaudiably...*

I'm-currently-engaged-to-the-sheriff?

LITTLE JOHN MARION?

FRIAR TUCK You're what?

MAID MARION As I said, long story, full of miscommunications but yes, I'm probably not the *best* person to smuggle out the dolls.

LITTLE JOHN What are we waiting for? Sounds like a SWEET plan to me, guys?

FRIAR TUCK It's genius!

LITTLE JOHN I've ALWAYS WANTED TO KNOW HOW TO SEW!

ALAN-A-DALE Well, just you be warned Marion, we don't want another girl bossing us about. Telling us what to do and what not.

MAID MARION Oh dear, well, bad news for you, Alan-a-Dale, because that's exactly what's about to happen.

7. Double Day

Characters: **SHERIFF, FRIAR TUCK, MAID MARION** *(dressed as choir boy).*

The scene then moves to Nottingham. The people of nottingham are terrified. Today is Double Day. And they know the **SHERIFF** *is livid. Big death march like drums. Sense of foreboding.*

[MUSIC NO. 9: "DOUBLE DAY"]

SHERIFF OF NOTTINGHAM
WE ALL KNOW WHAT TIME IT IS-
DOUBLE DAY, DOUBLE DAY,
UNTIE YOUR PURSE, UNCLENCH YOUR FIST
DOUBLE DAY, DOUBLE DAY,
YOU CANT HIDE OR RUNAWAY
DOUBLE DAY, DOUBLE DAY,
IT'S DOUBLE DAY SO PAY PAY PAY!
DOUBLE DAY, DOUBLE DAY,
BOOOOO, HISSSSSS (AUDIENCE JOIN IN)
THE STAKES ARE HIGH, THE RENT IS HIGHER,
DOUBLE DAY, DOUBLE DAY,
WITHIN OUR TOWN WE DO CONSPIRE,
DOUBLE DAY, DOUBLE DAY,
I LIKE TO DO THINGS MY OWN WAY
DOUBLE DAY, DOUBLE DAY,
BY TAKING YOUR BENEFITS AWAY,
DOUBLE DAY, DOUBLE DAY,
BOOOOO, HISSSSSS
THE HAND IS TICKING ON THE CLOCK,
DOUBLE DAY, DOUBLE DAY,
TAX COMES IN TWOS LIKE A PAIR OF SOCKS,
DOUBLE DAY, DOUBLE DAY,
I'M GENEROUS I'D LIKE TO SAY,
DOUBLE DAY, DOUBLE DAY,
BUT I CAN'T SO PAY, PAY PAY!

The SHERIFF *begins collecting his double tax from the poor. The* FRIAR *and* MARION, *in disguise as a choir boy, are handing out the dolls.*

SHERIFF OF NOTTINGHAM Good day to you Friar, doing your good work I see –

The FRIAR *looks nervous.*

FRIAR TUCK Ah yes, you know me, what with the double tax I –

SHERIFF OF NOTTINGHAM I suppose you've heard my good news?

FRIAR TUCK What good news?

SHERIFF OF NOTTINGHAM Don't pretend it's not the headline of every magazine – I'm doing it aren't I?

FRIAR TUCK Doing...?

SHERIFF OF NOTTINGHAM Getting married, of course we will want you to lead the ceremony –

FRIAR TUCK Oh, oh, yes of course. CONGRATULATIONS to you Sheriff.

SHERIFF OF NOTTINGHAM And who is this then?

The SHERIFF *points to* MARION, *dressed as the choir boy. The* FRIAR *is nervous.*

FRIAR TUCK Errr...my new choir boy, Sheriff.

SHERIFF OF NOTTINGHAM Choir boy? Well he'll have to sing at my wedding.

FRIAR TUCK I don't think he will be –

SHERIFF OF NOTTINGHAM I insist, let's hear you do a few notes then child...

MAID MARION Errr –

FRIAR TUCK He's on voice rest, he...

SHERIFF OF NOTTINGHAM Nonsense! How often do you get to sing at a Sheriff's wedding, once in a lifetime opportunity for the boy, come on, give us a little flavour.

FRIAR TUCK He will sing at your wedding I'm sure but honestly, we are visiting the poor today Sheriff, perhaps when he's in better spirits?

SHERIFF OF NOTTINGHAM SING!

> **MAID MARION** *awkwardly hits a few screechy off notes that sound terrible – The **SHERIFF** joins in and the two begin to sing together. The **SHERIFF** loves it. Relief from the **FRIAR**.*

Voice of an angel. You will have to be there at the wedding, a voice like that I want you right up the front with me – what are these?

> *The **SHERIFF** points to the dolls. Tension as the **SHERIFF** snatches one of **MARION**'s dolls with the coin stuffed into its back and inspects it.*

FRIAR TUCK Errr...dolls. For the children, Sheriff...as a donation, a gift, to lift their spirits.

SHERIFF OF NOTTINGHAM Well they aren't very well made are they? Still, I suppose it's better than hugging a dying ferret found on the roadside. Good work Friar Tuck. I suppose today is Double Taxes so let's be extra charitable. All about the children isn't it?

> *The **SHERIFF** pats **MARION**'s head, as though he loves children, and her choir boy bowl cut wig slips off in the **SHERIFF**'s hand. Her huge plaits tumble out. **MARION** turns to run but the **SHERIFF** catches **MARION** and launches her high into the sky. Hoisting her up by her plaits. The **SHERIFF** is genuinely shocked and hurt.*

Marion? I can't believe you? Why don't you want to marry me? I'm a nice guy really.

MAID MARION You're not! You're a BULLY! I will NEVER marry you!

MARION *spits in the* **SHERIFF**'s *face.*

SHERIFF OF NOTTINGHAM OH NO, NO, NO, NO. MY BRIDE! YOU'RE COMING WITH ME! AND YOU WILL PAY. YOU WILL ALL PAY!

The **SHERIFF** *addresses the audience too, all of Nottingham.*

As you all know today is Double Day and there is going to be a very big celebration aka MY WEDDING. You will all be expected to be ready at my castle by noon. And whoever brings me the special guest of honour, Robin Hood, will be exempt from taxes. And if you don't the next tax collection will be TRIPLE TAX and then FOURPLE ... TAX ... SO ... SO SOMEBODY BETTER BRING HER TO ME! And bring cake, bring cake too.

The **SHERIFF** *turns to leave.*

Except fruit cake. Don't like it.

8. The Brave Lionheart

Characters: **FRIAR TUCK, SHERIFF, MAID MARION, ROBIN HOOD, LITTLE JOHN, WILL SCARLET, ALAN, FRIAR.**

Big trumpets, sound of ceremony commencing. A parade. **WILL SCARLET** *is prepared to be hung with a noose around his neck, gag over his mouth.*

Enter the **SHERIFF** *and his bride,* **MARION**. *Looking not so happy. The* **FRIAR** *stands at the front, leading the service.*

FRIAR TUCK Ladies and gentleman, boys and girls, brothers and sisters, cousins an –

SHERIFF OF NOTTINGHAM Get on with it, blah, blah, blah, skip to the end, you are married.

FRIAR TUCK That's not how it works I'm afraid Sheriff.

SHERIFF OF NOTTINGHAM Well it is today, half of this lot will be asleep by the time this thing's done...got my Aunt Dot already dozing off, Dot, Dot, WAKE UP! SERIOUSLY?

FRIAR TUCK We are joined here today to...we are joined here today to...witness the matrimony of The Sheriff of Nottingham and Miss Maiden Marion –

MARION *begins to cry.*

Don't cry Marion.

SHERIFF OF NOTTINGHAM Tears of joy aren't they my *Beloved Hot Dog*? Messenger, could I get my recorder please? I'd love to play a love ballad to my sweet prin – Messenger, where is my Messenger? Meant to be my Best Man...can't even hand me my instrument! Where is he?

FRIAR TUCK Oh, we should probably wait for him before we –

SHERIFF OF NOTTINGHAM No, no, no, he's probably just preparing some sort of OUTRAGEOUS and CRAZY Best

Man prank for me somewhere isn't he? Cor, what's he like, eh? Carry on...

FRIAR TUCK Here, with you guests present, we –

SHERIFF OF NOTTINGHAM Come on, come on, get to the good bit.

FRIAR TUCK It's not all about, the kiss, Sheriff.

MAID MARION Please NO!

SHERIFF OF NOTTINGHAM Eugh. No not the kiss. YUCKY!

FRIAR TUCK Which bit then?

SHERIFF OF NOTTINGHAM The END!

FRIAR TUCK You cannot rush the vows of marriage.

SHERIFF OF NOTTINGHAM I wanna get on with this so that I can celebrate by hanging that *UNICORN-HEADED CRUMPET* over there don't I? It's ALL too exciting.

   WILL SCARLET *struggles...*

FRIAR TUCK Well, it's not for everyone but there is a Fast Track version of marriage?

SHERIFF OF NOTTINGHAM Yep. Love it. Bring it on. Love me a Fast Track.

MAID MARION Friar, *PLEASE* ... DON'T.

SHERIFF OF NOTTINGHAM Let's just get this whole thing wrapped up already. Am I right people? Can't wait for my first creamy dreamy EggNog with my future wife to be.

FRIAR TUCK In that case... From the top: Have, hold, better, worse, richer, poorer, sickness, health, love, cherish, till death us do part, vow, vow, ring, ring, I now pronounce you... HUSBAND AND WIFE! You may now kiss the bride!

MAID MARION No, no please, I really – really don't want to –

   Suddenly, **ROBIN** *swoops down to the scene.*

SHERIFF OF NOTTINGHAM ROBIN HOOD!

MAID MARION BIT LATE!

ROBIN holds her bow out ready to shoot the **SHERIFF**.

SHERIFF OF NOTTINGHAM You can't kill a man on his wedding day.

ROBIN HOOD I can do whatever I want.

SHERIFF OF NOTTINGHAM And what is it you want?

ROBIN HOOD Free Will Scarlet, take me instead.

MAID MARION Robin, no, don't.

SHERIFF OF NOTTINGHAM INSTEAD? Why instead when I have you both now? *NUUUUUUUHH!* It's DOUBLE DAY, TWO FOR THE PRICE OF ONE! Guards. Seize her!

ROBIN HOOD NO! You've wanted me for too long, think about it, Sheriff...

SHERIFF OF NOTTINGHAM Thought about it. BYE.

The **GUARDS** *surround* **ROBIN**. *The* **SHERIFF** *snatches* **ROBIN**'s *bow and arrow.* (**FRIAR** *exit*).

I'll be taking that, thank you.

The **GUARDS** *take* **ROBIN** *off, hanging up next to* **WILL SCARLET**.

That's it, hang her next to her traitor, right up close there, thaaaat's it...nice n close, go on, cheek to cheek with the old Will Scarlet. Little more to the left, right, back, up, smidgen to the left again...oooo back a bit, that's it, that's perfect. Oh I just LOVE me a DOUBLE DAY. Weddings, murders, two finger Kit Kats. Don't they look lovely Marion, my darling?

The **SHERIFF** *grabs* **MARION**.

In the mean time... Robin, you *Dainty Little Hand-Painted Pepper Pot,* you've got yourself into such a pickle. Risking your life for somebody who pretty much hates you.

ROBIN *looks at* WILL, *hurt.* WILL *cries.*

Oh, whoopsie, didn't somebody tell you? Aww, sorry.

ROBIN HOOD It's my fault he ended up here.

SHERIFF OF NOTTINGHAM Will betrayed you. Quick as a flash
he threw you right under the 137 bus all the way to Coventry.

ROBIN HOOD No, never. My Merry Many would NEVER betray
me.

SHERIFF OF NOTTINGHAM Oh they would. Just like how you're
about to be betrayed again, by your own bow and arrow,
when I shoot it RIGHT THROUGH YOUR GORGEOUSLY-
CREATED PERFECTLY-SHAPED HEART!

The SHERIFF *steadies the bow and arrow.*

Bear with me, I've never actually used one of these before,
not sure how they exactly work...oh harder than they look,
I see, well...no bother, if I can just...

LITTLE JOHN *and* ALAN-A-DALE *appear, swarm down,
both screaming like Tarzans.* ALAN *launches down and
snatches back* ROBIN's *bow and then cuts* WILL SCARLET
free, and LITTLE JOHN *swoops up* ROBIN.

No, no, no... NO YOU DON'T! THIS IS **MY** PARTY! THIS
IS NOT HOW IT GOES.

ROBIN, *now free, stands up on her feet with the bow and
arrow pointing at the* SHERIFF.

ROBIN HOOD Free Marion and you can take me in her place.

MAID MARION Robin, don't.

SHERIFF OF NOTTINGHAM It's too late, You *Prize-Winning
Turnip*! WE'RE ALREADY MARRIED.

MAID MARION Don't be ridiculous, of course we're not married,
there's no such thing as a 'fast track' wedding you fool, The
Friar would never marry me to you.

SHERIFF OF NOTTINGHAM Oh, what was that back there then...? Did that mean NOTHING to you?

SHERIFF *looks around, almost to 'production team'.*

Just words, was it? Words. Rings. Nothing? For real? Un-bel-ievable. Well that's that then. Our marriage is a sham.

ROBIN HOOD Free Marion and you can have me.

SHERIFF OF NOTTINGHAM Oh seriously spare me. We still on this? Robin, life is not just 'exchange student' after 'exchange student', you can't just run around swapping your lives for people. Life doesn't work like that.

ROBIN HOOD Let Marion go!

SHERIFF OF NOTTINGHAM Gosh, sorry I don't know why I'm laughing but I just thought of like the *funniest* thing. Imagine, Robin, if we just did something like...totally wild right now and WE got married, I mean, the set up's all here and I'm sure the Friar is still lurking round somewhere, could you imagine how random that would be? OH TRAA-LAAA *guess what guys, we're married,* ha, like just for MEGA LOLS or whatever...

MAID MARION Robin, don't, you can do more than I can out there, run whilst you can. You're a hero. You're no use in a prison cell.

SHERIFF OF NOTTINGHAM Hero? Oh, please, don't pretend you're her friend now. You told me yourself, you're not Robin's friend.

MAID MARION No, no –

SHERIFF OF NOTTINGHAM Oh yes, Mrs Sheriff of Nottingham, yes I recall you clearly saying you weren't her friend, you don't have to lie Sweetheart. Robin, all these people you're risking your life for, well, they seem to HATE you T.B.H.

ROBIN *looks hurt.*

MAID MARION Robin, don't listen to him, it's not true.

SHERIFF OF NOTTINGHAM Think you'll find it is Robin. Seems like you have absolutely zero smero nobody in this world at all...yikes. NAH, NAH, NAH, NAH, NAH. NO FRIENDS, NO FRIENDS, NO FRIENDS, COME ON GUYS, LET'S CHANT, NO FRIENDS ... NO ...

Nobody chants.

Oh stuff you then!

The **SHERIFF** *runs with* **MAID MARION** *...a sword digging into her back.*

MAID MARION ROBIN! RUN!

LITTLE JOHN Just shoot him Robin.

ROBIN HOOD I can't. He's right. I've got no friends. I've got no one.

LITTLE JOHN What are you talking about, you've got me.

ALAN-A-DALE And me.

FRIAR TUCK And me.

WILL SCARLET And me. If you'll have me. Sorry Robin.

LITTLE JOHN And all your other Merry Many...right guys?

To audience.

Go on Robin, you've always had our backs and this time, we've got yours. Shoot him. Kill him down dead.

SHERIFF OF NOTTINGHAM ROBIN, ROBIN, YOU PERFECT STACK OF FLUFFY SUNNY CIRCLES OF BUTTERMILK PANCAKES WITH BLUEBERRIES AND CREAM, YOU HAVE IRRITATED ME FOR THE FINAL TIME, I ACCEPT YOUR OFFER, I'LL TAKE YOUR LIFE FOR THE LIFE OF WHOMEVER YOU'D LIKE –

ROBIN *targets the* **SHERIFF.**

ALAN-A-DALE She's doing it! She's gonna kill the Sheriff! BRILLIANT!

ROBIN HOOD THIS, Sheriff, is for the people of Nottingham. MERRY CHRISTMAS!

ROBIN *shoots off* **SHERIFF**'s *little pinky finger.*

SHERIFF OF NOTTINGHAM OWWWWWW, that's my recorder finger!

MARION *runs free from his grasp.*

GAH! Guards... OFF WITH THEIR HE – oh no, no, no... it's him...it's him...he's here... Ahhhh, quick, quick, pass me a difficult looking novel or something, I need to look like I'm behaving myself –

They all turn up towards the sky. Smiling.

ROBIN HOOD IT'S HIM! I can't believe it.

MAID MARION OH MY –

LITTLE JOHN SANTA! SANTA! OVER HERE! I'M HERE! DID YOU GET MY LETTER?

ROBIN HOOD That's not Santa, Little John, it's King Richard, the Brave Lionheart. He's back, he's come back home!

9. Best Man Speech

Characters: **SHERIFF, GUARD** *(plus video footage of* **MESSENGER***).*

SHERIFF *sits in his cold, dark, damp, prison cell, quivering, playing a prison song.*

A **GUARD** *walks past.*

GUARD A package for you.

SHERIFF OF NOTTINGHAM For me?

Shocked, the **SHERIFF***, snivelling and shivering reaches out his hand and claws for his parcel. Lights down. It's a best man video from the* **MESSENGER***. He's on a beach in Hawaii, sunglasses, shades, cocktail in hand...the video plays...*

MESSENGER 'ello mate, sorry for the delay, SO here I am YOUR BEST MAN! Just a quick one to so sorry I couldn't be there, I ended up going to... HAWAII instead, it was a last minute thing...an offer, I obviously could not turn down. You could almost see it like our stag if you wanted to – LADS! LADS! LADS! No, not really, I'm just at my Nan's house really.

He steps out of the 'beach' scene...

She does a roast on a sunday so... Anyway just wanted to say... I hope you have a DIABOLICAL wedding day. And I hope Maid Marion runs away as far as she can from you, cos well, you're the absolute worst. I hope that Robin Hood bursts in when you least expect it and shoots you right where it hurts most with her bow and that... I don't know, King Richard comes back and frees ALL the helpless people whose life you have made such a misery and takes away the taxes and THROWS YOU, YOU UTTER VOMIT CHEESECAKE-FACED, SPINELESS, UGLY, HATEFUL, EGOTISTICAL, MEAN, CRUEL, HEARTLESS, SLITHERY,

COLD, CRUEL, TOO-TIGHT-SHORT-WEARING, BULLY TYRANT INTO A PRISON CELL. FOR THE REST OF YOUR AWFUL LIFE. NOW *THAT'S* HOW YOU OFFEND SOMEONE, PROPERLY? ALRIGHT. Such an emotional wedding, though, honestly even the cake's in tiers. I resign. You're an idiot. AND 28 IS A TERRIBLE TERRIBLE GOLF HANDICAP. PEACE.

Trembling, sobbing, the SHERIFF *opens up a card, he opens the card with a sense of hope, like it might have something better to say. The card opens and glitter explodes, out, everywhere and the* SHERIFF *wails.*

Finish with Kazoo's play to **"OUTLAW THEME MUSIC"**

The End

PROPS

ACT 1

Umbrella
Leaves
Wanted posters
Cloak
Watch
Purse
Fake cakes and food on tray
Throw
Declaration document and quill
Bags
Disguises
Kids trolley
Coconuts
Golden Carriage
Hat
Presents
Quiver
Mayoral Chain
Mounted Bear's head
Wine in leather pouch
Compact Mirror
2 x beer bottles and mug
Wheely chair and leg rest
Plastic Coins
Recorder
Harmonica
Scout camping equipment
Reward prices
Stream
Rubber Ring
Inflatable Crocodile
Bow and arrows

Inflatable Octopus
Bottles
Motorway sign
Map
Binoculars
Rucksack
Arm Bands
Fish on a stick
Snorkel and Goggles
Swords x 2
Money bags
Kazoos
Megaphone
Handcuffs
Whistle
Party Blowers

ACT 2

Bucket of water
Door Bell pully
Castle flag
Bunting
General knitting, crochetting
Tea tray
Cushions
Ragdolls
Wicker basket
Tea pot and tea cups
Shackles
Torch
Prison bars
Bag of frozen peas x2
Box of chocolates
Bouquet of roses
Basket

Plastic Coins
Wedding decorations
Finger Arrow
Nooses x2
Arrow Trick
Rope
Ken Doll and Mirror ball
Confetti Box
Film
Video and player
TV stand
TV

VISIT THE
SAMUEL FRENCH
BOOKSHOP
AT THE
ROYAL COURT THEATRE

Browse plays and theatre books, get expert advice and enjoy a coffee

Samuel French Bookshop
Royal Court Theatre
Sloane Square
London
SW1W 8AS
020 7565 5024

Shop from thousands of titles on our website

 samuelfrench.co.uk

 samuelfrenchltd

 samuel french uk

Lightning Source UK Ltd.
Milton Keynes UK
UKHW020402281118
333082UK00006B/718/P